OKEFINOKEE ALBUM

OKEFINOKEE
A·L·B·U·M

FRANCIS HARPER & DELMA E. PRESLEY

THE UNIVERSITY OF GEORGIA PRESS · ATHENS

The University of Georgia Press
Athens, Georgia 30602

Set in Mergenthaler Goudy Old Style

Design by Richard Hendel

Printed in the United States of America

Library of Congress Cataloging in Publication Data

Harper, Francis, 1886–1972
Okefinokee album.
Bibliography.
1. Okefenokee Swamp—Social life and customs.
2. Okefenokee Swamp—Description and travel.
3. Natural history—Georgia—Okefenokee Swamp.
4. Harper, Francis, 1886–1972.   I. Presley,
Delma Eugene, joint author.   II. Title.

F292.05H37   975.8'7504   80-14220
ISBN 0-8203-0530-8

Okefinokee Album
*is dedicated to Jean, who
faithfully has shared her husband's
love for the great swamp.
Robin, David, Molly, and Lucy keep the faith.
The book also is dedicated to Beverly,
who caught her husband's swamp fever
and gave it to three young friends of
the Okefinokee–Worth, Susan, and Edwin.*

CONTENTS

ix
Preface

xiii
Acknowledgments

xv
A Note on the Spelling of Okefinokee

xvii
Map

1
FRANCIS HARPER AND THE
PEOPLE OF THE GREAT SWAMP
An introduction by Delma E. Presley

31
THE WAY TO BILLYS ISLAND
*Francis Harper's account of his first journey to
the heart of the swamp*

51
OKEFINOKEE SAMPLER
*A miscellany compiled by Delma E. Presley from
the papers of Francis Harper*

OKEFINOKEE FOLK 53

POTIONS, PORTENTS, BALLADS, AND TALES 95

OKEFINOKEE ALBUM 111

SWAMP TALK 135

OF MAMMALS AND BIRDS 147

CHESSERS ISLAND JOURNAL, 1922–1951 165

181
NOTES ON A VANISHING BREED
A postscript by Delma E. Presley

191
Works on the Okefinokee

This book is about one of America's most fascinating natural areas. But it concerns more than the landscape and the creatures of Georgia's great swamp. It is an intimate view of the "land of trembling earth," focused through the eyes of the people who knew it best—the Okefinokee folk. It is a faithful recording of the most enchanting sound ever heard among the cypress bays and prairie heads—the sound of human voices at home in a dark, green wilderness.

A handful of Georgia's pioneering settlers ceased pushing westward and claimed the Okefinokee Swamp as their own around 1850. These independent frontiersmen established sturdy homes and productive farms as they developed a distinctive way of life in southeastern Georgia's most isolated area. Yet in less than a century the descendants of those original settlers were forced to abandon what the first generations had gained. The end of this community began in 1937 when the United States Congress declared the Okefinokee a national wildlife refuge. Today the swampers are gone and nearly forgotten.

Until now the story of the Okefinokee folk has been one of that region's deeper mysteries. We owe a debt of gratitude to Francis Harper, who preserved some of the essential records of that culture. This legacy started in 1912 as scribblings, afterthoughts, by a young Cornell naturalist on a biological reconnaissance. He was amused by the people he met, and he preserved bits of their conversation, perhaps out of idle curiosity. But in a few years amusement gave way to respect, and respect to admiration. Again and again he came back to the swamp—visiting backwoods friends, living as they lived, learning and sharing secrets of nature. "If all that I've seen in the Okefinokee was put in a book," Allen Chesser said in 1922, "it'd be right interesting. An' the pretty part of it, every bit of it's the truth." A lot of what this native swamper saw from the Civil War to the late 1920s appears in this book, and much more from other Chessers, and from Lees, Thrifts, Mizells, Roddenberrys, Hendersons, Spauldings, Gibsons, Coxes, Crewses, and others as well.

Harper wrote the last entry in his Okefinokee notebooks in 1951, after he had stopped for a brief visit and a meal with the Chessers. He was shaken by the enormous changes that had occurred in the swamp and in the swampers since he had started his first notebook in 1912. Harper had long wanted to write a book about his swamp friends. The experience of 1951 gave him resolve.

As early as 1920 Harper had considered writing a volume he wanted to call "The Okefinokee Folk." He had worked toward that end, off and on, throughout his life, particularly after the swampers were forced to move from the refuge area. The naturalist published over one hundred books, articles, essays, and reports, but he never completed the task he said was his most important. He left undone his tribute to the community that flourished in Georgia's great swamp from the 1850s through the 1930s. The Okefinokee project was yet to be completed when Francis Harper died on November 17, 1972.

Providence led me to the widow and sons of Francis Harper in May 1975. Only a few weeks earlier, my friend and former colleague John Bozeman had told me about his long talks with Harper at Chapel Hill, North Carolina, in the late 1960s. Knowing of my interest in Georgia Crackers and their heritage, John shoved an address into my hand and urged me to write to Jean Harper about using the files of her late husband. I did so right away, and for over three years I was privileged to work closely with the Harpers, who have become friends of my family.

When we borrowed the Okefinokee collection from Jean Harper, it was in three large cardboard boxes that consumed almost every inch of the trunk space of my wife Beverly's Plymouth Duster. From the start it was clear that the job of comprehending, sifting, and arranging the material was no small one. As I worked with the collection I realized that I was to be Harper's collaborator as well as his editor. The thirty-eight volumes of notebooks on the swamp, which he had diligently kept from 1912 to 1951, are the foundation for this volume, but they were not written with the thought that they would be published in that form. In many cases, then, I have had to weave fragmentary observations into sentences and to smooth transitions between paragraphs. Portions of the *Okefinokee Album* have been taken directly from Harper's material. Francis Harper speaks for himself in "The Way to Billys Island" and the "Chessers Island Journal." In the "Okefinokee Sampler" I have woven Harper's primary material into a sampler of the swamp's heritage. Here, from the pages of the notebooks, the swampers speak for themselves, recounting their tales in the frontier dialect that Harper knew was dying. We should be grateful that he never condescended to correct their grammar. In other cases I have gleaned Harper's material for the background to introduce the swamp and its people and to compile the "Swamp Talk" glossary. All of the photographs that appear in this volume were taken by Francis and Jean Harper. Together with the notebooks they form an unequalled record of another time.

Although Francis Harper never completed a draft of a manuscript, he had made notes about his plans. He had envisioned a volume much larger and more scholarly than this one—an omnibus of folklore, folk and popular music, biographical sketches, biological observations, word studies, drawings, and photographs. Such a large book, designed to please a multitude of interests, perhaps would have satisfied few. I also believe that it would not have served his desire to write a book that his friends in the swamp would cherish. I like to think that Francis Harper would have been pleased with this *Okefinokee Album*. During his career he found time to write for the layman, and his standards for popular writing have guided my effort.

In the introduction, "Francis Harper and the People of the Great Swamp," I recount Harper's career as it touched on the Okefinokee. But his work in the swamp was only one of his many professional commitments. The list of his publications near the end of this book is an indication of the breadth of his interests. A brief chronology of his professional career is another. A man of great energy, Harper often had more than one project under way. While completing his graduate studies at Cornell, he gained field experience by working for the geological survey of Canada and the United States Biological Survey. His graduate studies were interrupted by service in the First World War. While completing his dissertation, he worked as an instructor in zoology at the University of Michigan Biological Station and as a field zoologist for the New York State Museum. Upon receiving his Ph.D. from Cornell in 1925, he became an employee of the Boston Society of Natural History. In 1929 he joined the staff of *Biological Abstracts* in Philadelphia, where he remained until 1935.

From 1930 until 1940 he served as a research associate with the American Committee for International Wild Life Protection and for the John Bartram Association. During this period the Harpers lived alternately in the Okefinokee on Chessers Island and in Swarthmore, Pennsylvania. He was a member of the editorial staff of the American Philosophical Society in Philadelphia from 1942 until 1944. After spending two years as an agent for the Reading, Pennsylvania, Public Museum and Art Gallery, he received support from the

United States Office of Naval Research and the Office of the Surgeon General of the Army. His task was to prepare detailed zoological reports of the Neultin Lake region in Keewatin, under the auspices of the Arctic Institute of North America. After completing his duties in 1949, he joined the staff of the E. N. Huyck Preserve, Rensselaerville, New York, where he served as resident naturalist until 1951. In 1953 he went to interior Ungava—his last extensive field trip; the results of this expedition were recorded in a number of papers published by the Museum of Natural History of the University of Kansas. After seeing his naturalist's edition of *The Travels of William Bartram* (Yale University Press, 1958) through publication, he turned his attention to his Okefinokee collection.

I never had the privilege of meeting Francis Harper, but I know this about him: he cherished the extraordinary common people of rural Georgia. At this point Francis Harper and I become colleagues. It was Harper's good fortune to live among the Okefinokee folk. It is my good fortune to present this book to a generation that is eager to preserve its natural and human heritage.

⨯ ACKNOWLEDGMENTS ⨯

Jean Harper and her sons, Robin and David, have been more than helpful. They have been editors, interpreters, and sources of information. Francis Harper's longtime friend and colleague, Ralph Palmer, has given me good advice from the beginning. Chris Trowell of South Georgia College read an earlier version of the manuscript and made helpful suggestions. His drafts of the maps for this volume included features peculiar to Harper's description of the swamp. Joan Moser made accurate transcriptions of the folksongs Harper recorded in 1944. Iris Tillman Hill and Karen Orchard of the University of Georgia Press improved the work, and I especially appreciate their efforts to be faithful to Harper's viewpoint.

Many individuals who live or have lived near the swamp have shared their time generously with me. I would like to thank members of the families of Tom Chesser, Hamp Mizell, Harrison Lee, and Lone Thrift. I would also like to express appreciation to Harry Chesser, Iva Chesser, Wade Chesser, Vannie Hickox, Susan Stewart, Luther Thrift, John Luther Thrift, Henry Crews, Jimmy Walker, Ralph Davis, and Will Cox. Folks Huxford, Lois B. Mays, John Egnal, John Bozeman, and Judith Schomber provided answers to important questions at various times. Liston Elkins took a special interest in the project until his death in 1979, and I especially appreciate his account of the case of Oliver Thrift. On several occasions, the senior naturalist at the Okefenokee Swamp Park, Eugene Cypert, clarified matters for me, as did John Eadie and his colleagues at the Okefenokee Wildlife Refuge. The staff of Camp Stephen Foster patiently answered my questions during our delightful week there. Robert Izlar explained the history of logging in the swamp. Elder Charles F. Wells continues to teach me about one of south Georgia's most influential religious groups, the Primitive Baptists. Sturgis McKeever, my colleague at Georgia Southern College, pointed me in the right direction when I became lost among the mammals and birds. I appreciate the assistance provided by the extraordinary anglers, Penton Rimes and Alton Brannen. Again, Steve Ellwood came to the rescue with his photographic skills.

Many of my students have tolerated my preoccupation with this project.

Gibbs Flanders spent a great deal of time reviewing and correcting transcripts of folksongs, and Michael Lee Goodson worked just as hard on the swampers' language. Kyle Adkins also obtained information from his neighbors in Charlton County, Georgia.

I appreciate the services provided by the Archive of American Folksong of the Library of Congress, the Georgia Historical Society, the Georgia Department of Archives and History, the University of Kansas Library, the University of Georgia Libraries, and Georgia Southern College Library.

I would like to thank the Faculty Research Fund of Georgia Southern College for providing needed supplies and equipment. I am especially grateful to Oliver Pearson, who supported this effort to complete a task left unfinished by his colleague and friend.

Delma E. Presley
Statesboro, Georgia

Early in this century, the United States Geographical Board made what I consider an unfortunate choice in decreeing that the official spelling would be Okefenokee. I doubt if it made an adequate review of the case before issuing its fiat. Col. Benjamin Hawkins, distinguished Indian commissioner in the early days of the Republic, noted that the name was derived from the Creek word *O-ke-fin-o-cau*. George White's authoritative *Statistics of Georgia* (1849) and *Historical Collections of Georgia* (1855) have *fin* for the middle syllable as does *Lippincott's Gazetteer* (1856). John R. Swanton's *Final Report on the De Soto Expedition Commission* (1939) once again prefers *fin*. Students of birds in the southern United States have shown a preference for *fin*: Arthur T. Wayne, *Birds of South Carolina* (1910); *American Ornithologists' Union Check-list of North American Birds* (1931); and Frank M. Chapman, *Handbook of Birds of Eastern North America* (1939). It may be added that a large proportion of the zoologists who have specialized in the swamp fauna (aside from those in state or federal employ, who are scarcely in the habit of questioning the decrees of higher authority) still maintain the time-honored spelling, Okefinokee. It would be gracious of the United States Geographical Board to see the same light.

> *Francis Harper*
> April 12, 1967

The Okefinokee Swamp Around 1925

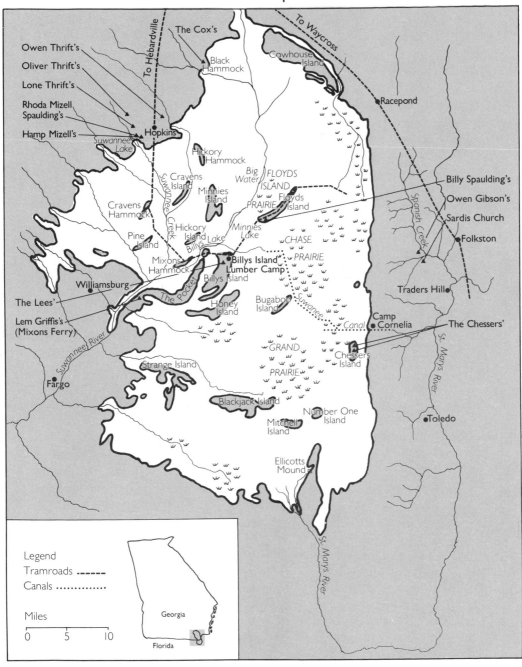

Owen Thrift's
Oliver Thrift's
Lone Thrift's
Rhoda Mizell
Spaulding's
Hamp Mizell's

The Cox's

To Hebardville
To Waycross

Black
Hammock
Cowhouse
Island

Racepond

Hopkins

Suwannee
Lake

Hickory
Hammock

Big
Water
FLOYDS
ISLAND
Floyds
PRAIRIE Island

Billy Spaulding's
Owen Gibson's
Sardis Church
Folkston

Cravens
Island
Minnies
Island

Cravens
Hammock

Suwannee Creek

Hickory
Island
Billys Lake
Minnies
Lake

Pine
Island

CHASE

Spanish Creek

Mixons
Hammock

Billys Island
Lumber Camp
Billys Island

PRAIRIE

Traders Hill

Williamsburg

The Lees'

Lem Griffis's
(Mixons Ferry)

The Pocket

Honey
Island

Bugaboo
Island

Suwannee

Canal

Camp
Cornelia

The Chessers'

St. Marys River

Suwannee River

GRAND

Chessers
Island

Fargo

Strange Island

PRAIRIE

Blackjack Island

Number One
Island

Toledo

Mitchell
Island

Ellicotts
Mound

St. Marys River

Legend
Tramroads ------
Canals ....

Miles
0   5   10

Georgia

Florida

FRANCIS HARPER
AND THE PEOPLE OF
THE GREAT SWAMP

An Introduction by Delma E. Presley

A NATURALIST AMONG THE SWAMPERS

Francis Harper was twenty-five years old when he first entered the great swamp as a junior member of a Cornell University biological survey team in May 1912. Even at this point in his career he was confident of his abilities as a naturalist. Like his colleagues, initially he was amused at the colorful habits and language of the Georgia Crackers who served as guides and cooks. He later admitted, however, that the swampers knew more about the flora and fauna of the Okefinokee than the team of researchers from the North would ever know.

Without exception Harper carefully kept field notebooks of his many trips to the region. These longhand records supplied data for his voluminous scientific publications and reports. Thirty-eight notebooks concern the swamp from 1912 through 1951. In the context of his larger collection of notebooks, these thirty-eight are remarkable, for they seem to have been written by a different Francis Harper—one far more concerned with people than with biology. The pages are filled with anecdotes, stories, songs, and ballads about people and about bears, 'gators, wildcats, and birds of the swamp. He also meticulously recorded what he liked to call the "Elizabethan quality" of the language he heard.

Over the years Harper observed the natives as they worked, played, rested, and worshiped. He copied local versions of traditional ballads such as "Barbara Allen" and "The Little Mohee," and songs that had had their origin in the region such as "Billys Island Boys" and "The Best Man in Charlton County." Even though he had been employed to collect specimens of swamp creatures for northern museums, he seemed equally interested in gathering folklore. One of his local assistants on Billys Island, at the heart of the swamp, wrote on March 17, 1917:

Hello Mr. Francis Harper
I am sending you some
Hides one crane unmasured

On other page.
Will copy Billys-
Island Boys later.
Will write a longer
letter soon.

                       Harrison Lee

The naturalist wrote down almost everything he heard the swampers say or sing, including those short tunes played at "frolics" (old-fashioned square dances) by fiddlers and banjo pickers. He particularly liked "The Catfish," "Sally Goodin'," and this colorful ditty:

Jaybird died of the whoopin' cough,
Bullfrog died of the cholic.
Jack came along with a fiddle on his back
And asked 'em all to the frolic.

The young man from Cornell soon came to love those people who sang, told stories, laughed, danced, and prayed, and he recorded their conversations, even their simple mealtime rituals, such as grace delivered heartily by Allen Chesser:

(slowly)   *Thank the Lord for what we have to eat.*
(rapidly) *Now, boys, turn up your plates. There's the hominy; hyere's the*
              gravy.

During his long and varied career Francis Harper had many scholarly projects underway, but he pursued the Okefinokee project passionately, although not always persistently. Often it seemed to be on the list of duties "to do next." For more than half a century, off and on, Harper worked with the swamp materials, and over the years he regaled his friends with lively conversations about the swampers. He especially enjoyed playing tape recordings of his favorite Okefinokee music—hollering. His deep personal interest in the Okefinokee project is revealed in this excerpt from a letter he wrote on April 5, 1970 to Iva Chesser, a member of one of the old-line swamp families: "I'll make sure that the book will be regarded as a distinct honor and credit to the swamp people. . . . The material I have in it can scarcely be duplicated, for the old timers who furnished it are now practically all gone. It will really be *their* book, telling of their lives and adventures in their delightful speech."

Harper, of course, was not the first outsider to observe sympathetically the swamp and its people. The American naturalist William Bartram, who had traveled in the region in the spring of 1773, wrote that it was a "most blissful spot of earth," a land full of Indian stories about things legendary and beautiful. Before Harper saw the dark waters of the Okefinokee, over a dozen journalists, naturalists, and writers had described, usually in passing, the life and times of the swamp and its pioneer settlers. Perhaps the earliest comprehensive introduction to the area was written in 1902 by Francis's older brother, Roland M. Harper. Seven years later the material appeared in a *Popular Science Monthly* article entitled "Okefinokee Swamp." Roland said of the Okefinokee: "Its almost untrodden islands, its dense moss-garlanded bays, and its broad open prairies, all have their peculiar charms, and must be seen to be appreciated. There is nothing else exactly like it in the world."

In more recent years the swamp has been the subject of a number of books. Several popular motion pictures have been filmed there, including "Swamp Water," which was based on the novel by Vereen Bell. And who can forget Walt Kelley's immortal characters in "Pogo"?

Many outsiders have written about the swamp, but Francis Harper came close to being an insider. The people there guessed he was up to something with all his note-taking and recording sessions, but they learned to accept their "neighbor's" peculiarities just as he tolerated theirs. In this way he honored one of the basic tenets of the Okefinokee code of conduct—respect for the opinions of others.

This is not to say that Harper's motives were always clear to the swampers. Because he was a naturalist by trade, the people assumed he was interested primarily in information about the flora and fauna, and they told him what they thought he wanted to hear: stories about their encounters with the swamp and its creatures. For this reason, surely, more than 80 percent of the material in his notebooks consists of animal-related stories. Harper's interest in the people themselves grew in time, and had he known more clearly his real subject when he collected his material, he might have sought additional information about the everyday lives of the swampers. As it stands, the collection contains less variety than it might have if Harper had been trained in folklore.

At first some people on Chessers Island distrusted Harper. They particularly did not like the way he quoted them verbatim in his publications. He spelled as he heard them speak. Someone might say to Harper: "If I was you." Harper would write down: "Ef ah wuz yer." Not surprisingly some swampers thought the naturalist was holding them up to ridicule. But Harper did not intend to make fun of his good friends. Indeed, he considered himself a Cracker, often pointing out that he had spent twelve of his boyhood years in the state of Georgia, where his family had moved from Southbridge, Massachusetts, in 1887, the year after his birth, and where his father had served as superintendent of public schools in Dalton and Americus until 1898. In time he was accepted by most of the Okefinokee folk. For instance, Susan Lee, born in 1920 on Billys Island, once wrote to Harper that her mother spoke of him "as a friend of the family . . . my mother always said that when you were at her home and left, she missed you as she missed her own boys."

Many of the natives grew fond of "that Francis" or "Mister Harper," and they enjoyed the company of Jean Sherwood Harper, whom Francis married in 1923, and their children, Molly, Robin, Lucy, and David. The Harpers adopted the Okefinokee custom of referring to older friends of the family as

The Harper family camp on Chessers Island, July 1931.

"Aunt" or "Uncle." (When the former Winnie Chesser wrote Mrs. Harper in 1978, she still addressed her in the manner of days past as "Aunt Jean.")

Research trips kept the Harpers away from the swamp more often than they liked. For several Christmases swamp families exchanged packages and cards by mail with their absent friends. When Harper lost his job as an editor of *Biological Abstracts* during the Great Depression, one of his swamp neighbors urged him to move his family into the swamp; later he offered to share half of his modest possessions. Although Harper did not accept the generous offer, he did move his family there and camped while building a cabin on Chessers Island in 1935–36.

By the mid-1930s Harper knew that the culture he had first observed two decades earlier was changing rapidly. One by one each winter the old timers who had sung so many songs and told even more stories were dying. He began to hear the sound of radios on islands deep in the swamp where music had once been made only by the residents. Children of the Okefinokee now were going to public schools in the nearby communities of Folkston, Waycross, Fargo, and Moniac, Georgia. Teachers encouraged the youngsters to unlearn their ways. Slowly but surely the Okefinokee culture was vanishing.

Ironically, by advocating successfully the creation of the Okefenokee Wildlife Refuge, Francis Harper hastened the removal of the swamp community. Although a number of influential citizens in Waycross and Folkston had attempted to persuade the federal or state government to protect the Okefinokee as early as 1916, they were not successful. After the American economy collapsed in the early 1930s, many sadly acknowledged that the dream would have to be deferred. After hearing rumors that developers were planning to build a ship canal through the swamp, Francis and Jean Harper decided to appeal directly to one of the nation's leading conservationists, President Franklin Delano Roosevelt.

Jean Harper had worked for the president as a tutor to his children Anna and Elliot at Hyde Park after she had graduated from Vassar College. On November 25, 1933 she wrote to her former employer and friend in Washington:

> Dear Mr. Roosevelt: There is a matter that needs your immediate attention—the preservation of the Okefinokee Swamp. Perhaps you may recall that a few years ago, Francis sent you some of his reprints on the Swamp. . . . For twenty odd years naturalists and nature-lovers have been working for the preservation of this marvellous wilderness; unique in its nature not

only in this country, but in the world. The character of its fauna, its flora, and its human life is unsurpassed.

Two years ago the Senate Committee on Wild Life Resources visited the Okefinokee and submitted a report (pursuant to S. Res. 246) recommending its purchase as a national wild-life refuge. But because of the depression, nothing further has been done.

We now learn of the project to put a ship canal through the swamp. You well know what this would mean to the beauty of the area and to the wild life. The destruction that would thus be brought on is unthinkable. Our hope lies in you to stop the project before it goes farther, and spend the money in the purchase of the swamp for a reservation, where beauty and scientific interest may be preserved for all time. . . .
Sincerely,
(Jean Sherwood Harper)

President Roosevelt responded on December 19, 1933, saying that he "should hate to see the Okefinokee Swamp destroyed." But he did not take the matter into his own hands until February 18, 1935, when he responded to another plea Jean Harper had made ten days earlier.

Dear Jean: The enclosed comes from Mr. Darling. I would be entirely willing to have it made a national monument but this would have to come through Congressional action. I am asking Mr. Darling to speak to the delegations concerned.
Always sincerely,
(Franklin D. Roosevelt)

Jean Harper had won the support of President Roosevelt, and he made the Okefinokee a special project. His official correspondence contains several letters and memoranda written from 1935 to 1937 to Jay N. Darling, Chief of the Biological Survey, Henry A. Wallace, Secretary of Agriculture, and Harold L. Ickes, Secretary of the Interior. The victory was won when the Okefenokee Wildlife Refuge was created by Executive Order 7593 of March 30, 1937. Extending over portions of Charlton, Clinch, and Ware counties in southeastern Georgia, the refuge now comprises approximately 400,000 acres.

Once the swamp became federal property, the Okefinokee community began to disintegrate. While some moved to small villages near the edge of the swamp, others took jobs in Savannah, Macon, and Atlanta. Those who stubbornly remained in their old homes gave up the struggle to support themselves as they always had when officials warned them that it was illegal to protect their cows and hogs by killing the menacing bears and wildcats. For a while Tom Chesser's family continued to live in their old homestead, but they found it impossible to keep livestock if the government forbade the use of firearms. A letter written on August 30, 1941 from Wade Chesser to Robin Harper reveals the hopelessness of their situation:

> Robin, as school and harvest time approach, things begin to get busy again. But the first thing I want to tell you about is the bears. They ate up nearly all my grandfather's hogs! He and some men killed one of the bears, and said there were three more. But yet the bad part of it is that they now have started eating our hogs. Last Sunday evening he caught two, but one got away somehow and came home all cut up. Mother doctored her and put cotton in the cuts. Now she is getting better. . . . Bears for the grown hogs and cows, and wild cats for the pigs. So the future looks pretty dark for stock.

Realizing that the Okefinokee way of life might soon be forgotten, Francis Harper was determined to preserve and organize his collection of notebooks, letters, photographs, and movies, and to continue to publish articles and reports about the swamp and its people. In 1926, he had published a significant article devoted to the folklore of the swampers, "Tales of the Okefinokee," in *American Speech*, and other publications followed. Jean Harper's article "Collecting Folk-Songs in the Okefinokee Swamp," which she had written for the *Vassar Quarterly* (February 1933), outlined some of their plans: "We hope soon to be able to publish the folk-songs, including the ballads, fiddle and banjo pieces, dance songs, and poems in the vernacular. We hope also to secure the music, so that the record will be complete and the full charm of the songs transmitted. So far no music has been recorded, owing to the lack of an instrument or someone to take down the music. But when all is gathered together, we feel that we shall have preserved for all time a collection worthy of these fine people."

In 1944 the Archive of American Folk Song in the Library of Congress awarded Francis Harper a small grant and loaned him a battery-powered disc recorder. Assisted by his son Robin, Harper spent several weeks in August 1944 visiting some of his old friends and arranging recording sessions. Unfortunately the recorder provided by the Library of Congress was broken during shipment. Several weeks passed while father and son awaited the arrival of a new part for the recorder. Finally they were able to record some fine examples of singing, hollering, and storytelling. Yet, as Harper knew, 1944 was a decade too late to capture the great voices of the swamp. By then the most accomplished instrumentalists and vocalists had died or were too old to perform.

Francis Harper had other professional commitments in the 1940s and 1950s that drew him away from his Okefinokee project. He completed the final volume on the findings of John and William Bartram for the American Philosophical Society in 1944. In 1945 he put finishing touches on his largest single work about animals, *Extinct and Vanishing Animals of the Old World*. He spent the next dozen years on arctic expeditions, wrote the required reports, and completed a naturalist's annotated edition of *The Travels of William Bartram*.

Francis and Jean Harper moved to Chapel Hill, North Carolina, in 1960, and he vowed to write his Okefinokee book. But he was not able to secure sufficient outside funding to carry on. His advanced age was a liability, and folklore had not yet gained widespread respect as a scholarly discipline. Still, he worked, and his enthusiasm grew as he used the excellent folklore holdings in the library of the University of North Carolina at Chapel Hill.

During the next decade Harper began to experience the infirmities of old age. He was unable to concentrate on his writing for long stretches of time and occasionally was in ill health. Other distractions arose. In 1970, then in his eighties, Harper began writing endless rounds of letters, arguing with colleagues and politicians about his social and political opinions. He stopped writing scholarly articles to engage in a vigorous letter campaign against the aerial spraying of the pesticide Mirex.

Writing "concerned reader" letters had been a specialty of Francis's older brother Roland before his death in 1966; Francis now took up where Roland had left off. Some of the last letters he wrote reveal that Harper's mind was beset with complaints about the dishonesty of politicians and the dangers of industrial pollution and racial integration. Only a small portion of the Okefinokee material was written during Harper's days of political bitterness. Occasionally he injected a conservative political comment into his discussion of swamp culture: "At any rate, life rolled on in the Okefinokee without regimentation, federal taxes, and the innumerable other vexations and frustrations that have so thoroughly permeated modern American living. . . . They were not softened by luxury nor misled by demagogues. Consequently they were independent in thought and action, and unhampered by labor unions, bucket shops, brain-washers, or racial crackpots" (April 17, 1968).

Harper clearly had strong feelings about centralized government, labor unions, and the civil rights movement: he opposed them all. In his last days he was obsessed with the failings he perceived in contemporary life. In the complexities of the modern day, he longed to recover that simpler culture he had experienced in the swamp in his younger years. Until the end Harper believed that he would live to see the swamp book in print, but his declining health and his other preoccupations conspired against it.

On his eighty-sixth birthday, November 17, 1972, Francis Harper died. Jean Harper's immediate thoughts were of her husband's unfinished work; somehow the Okefinokee book would be completed, she thought, as she carefully preserved the materials from Georgia. Faced with miscellaneous notes, files, negatives, letters, and memorabilia, she worked diligently to bring a book on the swamp folk to realization.

The collection gathered by Jean Harper reveals the hours of painstaking labor Harper had devoted to the swamp material in his last years. Transcripts of songs, ballads, and stories are meticulous copies of original material contained in his field notebooks, most of which exist in very good condition. Notes from the *Oxford English Dictionary* on clues to archaic swamp expressions and from other reference works on analogues to swamp music are among the papers. And he had preserved his large collection of photographs and negatives.

Although Francis Harper did not live to complete his work, what remained spoke of the man and his intent. He had carefully recorded and preserved all that he had experienced in the Okefinokee, but more important, he had captured the spirit of the swampers and passed on the knowledge and the wisdom of the way of life he had shared with them. Ultimately he wanted the readers of his Okefinokee book to consider their philosophies of life in a materialistic age. In important ways the people of the Okefinokee had persuaded Francis Harper to reconsider his approach to people and to nature itself. They had taught him to be more human, he felt, and to be more concerned with the deeper values of life; he experienced this awareness in small, often unnoticed, moments of communion with his swamp friends.

The achievement of the swampers, Harper wrote on April 17, 1968, was not small:

They exemplified the kind of life extolled by Horace in his noble lines on the prisca gens mortalium. *Would that we might yet turn back the pages of history and lead once more such a simple, wholesome, abundant life! But what hope is there, while we abandon spiritual freedom in favor of creature comforts? Some of the finest days of my whole life have been spent in the pleasant company of such friends as the Lees, the Chessers, the Mizells, and the Thrifts. They were such keen observers of nature that I have felt privileged to fill many pages of my biological writings with verbatim comments of theirs on the wildlife of the swamp. Some of their observations have exceeded those of professional naturalists. I have often remarked that they contributed far more to my biological knowledge than I have to theirs; also that they are more genuine friends than the majority of people I have known. In other words, they have been friends for friendship's sake—not for any ulterior motive. . . . All told, I should say that both Georgia and the nation owe a real debt of gratitude to the wonderful Okefinokee people.*

Francis Harper also deserves a good measure of gratitude. He perceived the unique dignity of the swampers and earnestly sought to understand them and gain their friendship; he preserved their voices and faces so that now we too may hear and see them. Surely, we can learn something in their presence and, thanks to Francis Harper, can enjoy the pleasure of their company.

Okefinokee Album is the story of the people who lived on the farms in and around the Great Swamp. To say that the swamp formed their character may be an overstatement, but the piney woods did seem to lend a distinctive flavor to their manners, customs, and speech, and these folk must have been affected by their isolated and somewhat primitive existence. And so, before turning to the swampers, whose songs and tales and lore assume a knowledge of the physical features of their land, we turn first to the swamp itself.

The Okefinokee basin is part of the Atlantic Coastal Plain, or, as Georgians call it, the "Flat Pine Barrens." The swamp is about 660 miles square and 120 feet above sea level and owes its existence to the famous Trail Ridge, which acts as a natural land dam along its eastern border. The dark waters are fed by half a dozen creeks on the northwestern side; the main outlet is the Suwannee River, which empties into the Gulf of Mexico, but some of the waters also drain by the St. Marys River into the Atlantic Ocean.

The Okefinokee's mystery, like its charm, is indestructible, and amazingly it has withstood disasters brought by nature and by man. Before settlers claimed the area, according to swamper Owen Mizell, the "big fire" of 1844 appeared to "burn up" the swamp. The smoke was so thick that it hung over the region like a tent for weeks; but instead of destroying the swamp the "big fire" removed so much underbrush and peat that several lakes were formed. Severe burning in the spring of 1932 helped to unclog a number of waterways. Five great fires ravaged the swamp in 1954 and 1955, and almost 360,000 acres, two-thirds of the total area, were burned. Paradoxically, within a few years the swamp not only overcomes natural disasters but is replenished by them.

On two occasions modern technology has been used by men to "reclaim" the Okefinokee, while the swamp has resisted their efforts with stubborn resilience. In 1889 the Suwannee Canal Company paid the State of Georgia 26.5 cents an acre for 380 square miles of the swamp, with the intention of draining the mucklands and connecting a central canal with the east-running St. Marys River. The giant virgin cypress timber could then be floated to sawmills near the Atlantic coast. The idea drew enthusiastic sup-

A timber company moved onto Billys Island, bringing with it lumberjacks, railroad men, and a new technology. This skidder, part of the timber operation of the Hebard Cypress Company, pulled logs from the swamp to be loaded onto railway cars. June 1921.

Fire ravaged the Okefinokee, but miraculously rejuvenated it. This photograph of the fire-blackened swamp was taken on Chessers Prairie in April 1933.

port from government agents and businessmen. By 1891 the company's leader, Captain Harry Jackson, had crews working around the clock gouging out channels 6 feet deep and 45 feet wide. But the more they dug, the more futile their efforts became. One employee of the company is said to have remarked to his boss: "If we's aimin' to put water into the St. Marys, why is it all running toward the Suwannee?" The ballyhooed commercial venture within a few years was nicknamed appropriately "Jackson's Folly." After the developer died in 1895, the Suwannee Canal Company ceased operation. Many of its steam engines and platforms were abandoned inside the swamp, where they quickly rusted and rotted.

Early in the twentieth century, ownership of most of the Okefinokee passed into the hands of the Hebard Cypress Company of Philadelphia. Instead of trying to change the essential nature of the swamp, these practical businessmen used another form of technology to strip away most of the treasured cypress. They fastened railroad tracks to wooden pilings and penetrated the wooded islands and bays. By the end of World War I the company was working at capacity. The governor of Georgia, Hugh Dorsey, glowingly described their operations in a letter of June 16, 1916 to Dr. Lucien L. Knight, director of the Georgia Department of Archives and History: "The Hebert Lumber Co. of Philadelphia . . . have, near Waycross, the largest cypress mill in the world. I am informed that enough timber is found in this swamp to last for a hundred or more years, if they should cut it night and day at the rate they are now going."

Quickly the timbermen cut their way through the swamp. In the 1920s nearly two thousand workers conducted lumbering and turpentining activities on the principal islands—Billys, Honey, Black Jack, and Floyds—islands that contained vast stands of primeval timber. The once-secluded Billys Island was the site of a hotel and a large store, within a stone's throw of the Lees' log home. A church, school, and movie theater were built to satisfy the demands of the five to six hundred people who worked on the island.

Governor Dorsey, however, was overly optimistic: the cutting did not last a hundred years; it did not last even a decade. By 1925 the company reduced its operations dramatically, having stripped Billys Island of its magnificent trees. The mill at Hebardville stopped operating in 1927, because owners of the company found it unprofitable to harvest the yet uncut gum, bay, and pine trees.

And so, the Okefinokee endures. It not only has survived but apparently has benefited from severe burnings. The devastation caused by man is not as obvious as it once was. The marks left by the "developers" are, for the most part, fleeting. The swamp has swallowed most of the implements left by timber cutters. It has healed the surface wounds inflicted by the turpentiners.

Today the Okefinokee appears much as it must have to William Bartram two centuries ago when he described it as "a most blissful spot of the earth" or to Francis Harper seven decades ago when he first journeyed to its heart. The piney woods, the swampy woods, and the waterways change but they endure.

THE PINEY WOODS

The wooded islands of the swamp, and the greater portion of the land adjacent to it, are known as the "piney woods." Here one finds hammocks, "sand scrub," and the stately longleaf, slash, and black pines. The pines once furnished material for two of the leading industries of the region—lumbering and turpentining—and the wire-grass and other herbage of the piney woods supplied grazing for the settlers' cattle and goats, while droves of hogs grew fat upon the natural crops of the woods. Here too were excellent hunting grounds for bear, deer, squirrel, rabbit, turkey, and other game.

The hammock is an oasis of hardwoods and shrubs within the piney woods. Here grow the live oak, water oak, laurel, red bay, sassafras, sweet gum, loblolly bay (a magnolia), and the saw palmetto. Some of the more prominent hammocks can be seen on the northern part of Chessers Island, on the southern third of Floyds Island, on the northern end of Billys Island, and on the island northeast of Cravens Lake. Cravens Hammock is notable in the annals of ornithology, for it was there, around 1913, that Sam Mizell secured an ivory-billed woodpecker that eventually found its way into the permanent collection of the Academy of Natural Sciences of Philadelphia. Apparently it is the only Okefinokee specimen of this very rare species that has been preserved in a museum.

On the southern half of Floyds Island is a distinctive growth called "sand scrub." It is noticeable because it seems to divide the piney woods from the hammock. Bare sand is evident everywhere, and it practically has no covering of humus. Aside from a few scattered pines, there is almost no timber of value to be found in the "sand scrub." Although there are similar areas elsewhere in the swamp, the sand scrub on Floyds Island is unique.

A beautiful collection of cypress bays and ponds, sphagnous bogs, and prairie "heads" creates the swampy woods. Cypress bays and sphagnous bogs must compose more than half the swamp. Water stands over the greater part of the bays in depths from an inch to a couple of feet, varying with seasonal rainfall. It is possible to travel within these bays, thanks to the "tussocks," or patches of humus rising above water level. Many bays contain "runs" or paths that can be navigated by small boats. Once these boats were propelled by poles or paddles; today the outboard motor is common. Swamp hunters were wonderfully adept at pursuing game through the "runs."

The denser cypress bays are places of deep shade and at times oppressive gloom, but there is a somber beauty here. The atmosphere is echoed in the deep, uncanny notes of the barred owl, and the presence of bats, parula and prothonotary warblers, pileated woodpeckers, cottonmouth moccasins, cricket frogs, green tree-frogs, otters, and raccoons.

Among the bogs and marshes called *prairies* (pronounced *per-rārie*) the traveler can find small wooded islands or *prairie heads*. These spots were once best known to trappers and alligator hunters who found them to be convenient camping-places; today some refer to them as *houses* or *thicks* (possibly short for thickets). Several examples of prairie houses used to be found easily on Grand Prairie in the vicinity of Buzzard Roost Lake; in many of them were those familiar clearings where the Okefinokee hunter made his lonely bivouac. Remains of old campfires, bleached skulls of raccoon, otter, and wildcat were strewn about, and perhaps there might be a hole dug down through the humus to make a shallow well. At times the bear also left his imprint—a bed of pressed-down dead leaves.

THE WATERS

The principal watercourses of the Okefinokee include the prairies and various creeks, rivers, ponds, and lakes. Okefinokee prairies are marshes or bogs that are largely covered with water and flourishing aquatic plants. Most of them are in the eastern half of the swamp, and they are usually separated from the islands or mainland by a narrow strip of cypress bay or sphagnous

The pitcher plant (Sarracenia minor) *grows nearly a yard high on the Okefinokee prairies—twice the height it's known to reach in other locales. May 1932.*

bog. Cowhouse, Floyds Island, Carters, Durdins, Territory, Chase, Christies, Mizells, Chessers, Grand, Honey Island, and Black Jack are prairies that compose roughly one-fifth of the swamp. The prairies define the typical Okefinokee scene. Watery vistas between moss-hung prairie "heads" have an especially appealing beauty; here are acres of white and yellow water lilies, widespreading ranks of yellow "hardhead" (*Xyris*), thick green beds of "maiden cane" (*Panicum*) sheltering diving grasshoppers; purple flowers of bladderwort rising from floating mosslike leaves, blue-flowered "wampee" (*Pontederia*) forming a border about every lake and 'gator-hole. And then there are the ferns, "never-wets," and "pitcher plants."

The chief outlets are the St. Marys and Suwannee rivers. There is also the ill-fated Suwannee canal which was abandoned in the 1890s on the eastern side of the swamp near Folkston. There are many lakes: Billys, Minnies, Dinner Pond, Cravens, Sego, Monkey, and Buzzard Roost. One lake is called simply Big Water, and there are also the well-traveled Minnies Lake Run and its connecting channels north and south, as well as other runs connecting several watercourses.

The 'gator-holes occupy deeper parts of the prairies, and they are believed to be kept free of vegetation by their namesakes. Most holes are 15 to 60 feet wide and 3 to 5 feet deep. Curious as it may seem, an occupied 'gator-hole is said to contain more fish than one in which no 'gator is present.

Swamp water is fairly clear but brown in color from the dissolved vegetable matter and the minute particles of peat suspended in it. Apparently free of both lime and mud, the water tastes excellent, though its temperature in summer leaves something to be desired for the thirsty traveler.

THE FARMS

The swamp itself remains much as it was when Francis Harper visited in the early years of this century. The quiet farms that flourished there, however, have gone. In earlier days rustic homesteads stood on the borders of the swamp and on Billys and Chessers islands. Land under cultivation between the eastern border of the swamp and the St. Marys River amounted to no more than 5 percent of the total area of the region. The principal crops of south Georgia grew well on the sandy soil: corn, cotton, sweet potatoes,

Jean Sherwood Harper and two of the Chessers navigate a boat run on Chessers Prairie. May 1930.

On the top is a home near Harris Creek, April 1932. On the bottom, a man at his well-sweep pours water into a decade-old cypress trough. The shelter behind him is for boiling cane syrup, June 1920. The quiet farms that flourished in the Okefinokee have not survived.

sugar cane, peanuts, field peas, watermelons, peaches, pecans, tomatoes, and a few other garden crops.

The farm homes were sturdy log cabins (not shacks) with durable roofs of cypress shingles. These comfortable dwellings were shaded by live oaks or Chinaberry trees. On Billys Island the Lees enjoyed several ornamental trees, including cabbage palmettos, orange trees, and a couple of sycamores. Almost every farm home had pecan and persimmon trees in its dooryard. Many families also maintained a flourishing scuppernong arbor which was as indispensable as a watermelon patch.

Much to its credit the Okefenokee Swamp Park near Waycross has restored several farm dwellings on Cowhouse Island. The Department of Interior is responsible for the restoration on Chessers Island, which is particularly significant, for it is an authentic reproduction of an entire farmstead, including the famous Chessers Island syrup shed. Now visitors to either swamp entrance—Waycross or Folkston—have an opportunity to observe these scenes of swamp life in earlier days.

Perhaps the uniqueness of the swampers was that they existed at all. The Okefinokee folk in 1912 lived as though they had been untouched by the changes that reshaped the nation after the Civil War. They were the last remnants of Georgia's pioneers, the Crackers. As early as the 1760s, their forebears started moving into the southern colonies, over the objections of the British loyalists. Most of them were Scots from Northern Ireland, or Scotch-Irish, though some had traces of English, Welsh, French, and German ancestry. These early settlers had remarkable courage. They were also as stubborn as they were strong.

One British official wrote that these bold outsiders were called Crackers, because they were "great boasters." Dictionaries of the period confirm that Cracker applied to "proud" or "boasting" individuals, particularly to the Scots. In Georgia's backwoods the Crackers were not unique. They belonged to that rolling tide of frontiersmen that swept across the South in the early 1800s.

The Hillbillies and Tar Heels of the Appalachians shared the Okefinokee Crackers' ancestry, speech, folklore, and social ways. Both the mountain and the swamp people lived in isolation from mainstream America, and they were able to preserve in part the cultural heritage of Britain. But nature was more genial in the swamp than in the mountains. The swampers had an abundance of game and fish, and they found it easy to raise crops in this flat country. The Okefinokee folk lived more carefree, comfortable lives than the mountaineers, and they were slower to adopt the so-called advantages of modern civilization.

Consider the example of Allen Chesser, who was born in the 1850s. As an adult he was accustomed to drive a span of oxen from his island to the county seat, a round trip of twenty miles. When he left home his cart was laden with furs, wild ducks, and cane syrup. He returned from town with powder and shot for his sons and himself. For his wife he would bring yard goods that she would turn into attractive clothing. Now and then he brought back a barrel of flour and other simple commodities. His first night from home would be spent with his neighbor David Mizell, who lived four miles out on the "hill" or mainland. Then he would drive his team to Traders Hill and return homeward after he had completed his business in three days. In the 1930s mules replaced oxen for transportation and farming, but life remained simple.

Even before the government took control of the swamp in the late 1930s, the baneful march of progress was evident everywhere. At the turn of the century bears roamed freely on Billys Island in the heart of the swamp. During World War I a timber company moved onto the island, bringing with it over two hundred lumberjacks, railroad men, and supervisors. The shrill sound of the buzz saw invaded the quiet haunts of the wildcat and the otter. In the evening the unfamiliar sounds of the lumber worker's radio split the still air and broke ageless rhythms of the swamp and its creatures. The Okefinokee would never again be the same.

Swampers naturally could not resist the advantages of modern living. In the early 1930s for some the electric light replaced the torch of "light'ood knots." The mechanical pump supplanted the graceful well-sweep. The temporary frame shack crowded out the sturdy log cabin of pleasant memory. Even the speech of lifelong residents poorly withstood the influence of outsiders. People who used to question visitors with "Do how?" learned to use the prosaic "What?"

The stories in the *Okefinokee Album* are rich with the regional vernacular. The everyday speech of the swampers is spiced with such delightful words as *betwixt* and *blowzy*, *fitified* and *flinder*, *gamet* and *gower*, and *passel* and *progue*. The "Swamp Talk" section of the book is a taste of their vocabulary. Many of their expressions have survived from frontier days; others, for instance their common names for the local wildlife, originated in the swamp and are peculiar to it.

The people cherished and developed the art of storytelling, and books, magazines, and newspapers seldom found their way into Okefinokee homes. Many wonderful tales were told around firesides and in camps by the older hunters, and there is poetry, philosophy, and humor in their stories.

Music was an important part of the life of the swamp. The Primitive Baptist churches kept alive the religious songs of earlier days, and some swampers knew by heart the contents of the songbook *Primitive Hymns*, published in 1841. Many also attended monthly "singings" at nearby churches; there they learned *The Sacred Harp*, a hymnal in which each tone of the scale appears as a differently shaped note.

On weekdays ballad singing was a popular pastime. "Barbara Allen," "Little Mohee," and other traditional ballads had been preserved by local singers.

Other ballads, such as the one about the Civil War draft evader Dan'l Spikes, originated in the Okefinokee and were composed by and about persons known by the singers.

In the late fall—the season of "hog-killin' and cane grindin'"—the old fashioned "frolic" with its square dancing and fiddling was the most popular entertainment. Frolics were held year round, but they reached their high point in the harvest season. When fiddlers were not busy playing for frolics, they performed their tunes before small audiences in their homes. One such artist, Rob Mizell, had the reputation of being able to play all day long without repeating a tune. The fiddlers generally taught themselves and played "by ear." Among the local favorites were "Sally Goodin'," "Cotton-eyed Joe," "Molly Put the Kittle On," and "One-eyed Gopher." Almost as popular as the fiddle was the banjo, and some of the most resonant banjos were made at home from animal hides stretched across the rims of worn-out flour sifters.

By far the finest of all musical gifts of the swampers was their "hollerin'." It is the ultimate art of yodeling, no more to be likened to the yodeling in country and western music than grand opera to the hurdy-gurdy. To be sure, hollering was the grand opera of the Okefinokee, and it was an art shared by man, woman, and child. Little has been written about this unique American music, although recently a form of the art has been revived at annual "hollering conventions" held at Spiveys Corner, North Carolina. "Hollerin'" has been heard in the rural districts of most southern states, but the swampers' art was special.

At times a "holler" was a spontaneous expression of sheer exuberance. At other times it was a hunter's signal to his family that he was bound for home. Swampers seemed incapable of driving cattle home without this beautiful accompaniment. The measured cadences of alternating head tones and chest tones gave the music a remarkable carrying power. Hollerers have been heard for several miles, their voices bouncing rhythmically off the still waters at daybreak and sundown.

How did the swampers view the human condition? To say they beheld life through Calvinistic lenses provided by the Primitive Baptist church would be correct but inadequate. They believed man to be an imperfect creature in need of salvation; yet man's imperfections were seen in the larger perspective of the goodness of God. The one who preaches this gospel, moreover, is not a professional clergyman but a layman who has been called to the office of "elder" by the "brethren." On weekdays he earns his bread as do the members of the congregation—"by the toil of the hands, by the sweat of the brow."

Hamp Mizell demonstrates his two-mile swamp holler.

A Lee family baptism in Billys Lake. May 1921.

Outsiders often have misunderstood the Primitive Baptists, assuming that such believers are backward, superstitious, or overly emotional. Actually they are nothing more than contemporary examples of the frontier American Baptists of the early nineteenth century. Whether the questions concern organized missions, church-supported seminaries, or musical instruments, Primitive Baptists tend to respond that "these things are foreign to the Bible and to the old ways."

For their stubbornness and deep-seated conservatism, they have become known as "hardshell" Baptists. They insist on using real wine at communion and on washing the feet of brothers- and sisters-in-the-faith, just as the New Testament commands. The adjective *primitive* means they are "original" in their faith and practice, the Primitive Baptists like to say.

The Okefinokee folk valued highly their community of distant neighbors and friends, and they relished the frolics and monthly Primitive Baptist church meetings that brought them all together. Yet they seemed to value even more highly the individuals who made up that larger community. They put a premium on what some have called "the inner life," and they assumed that wise people cultivated that part of life as a matter of course.

It is important to notice that people whom society often labels "nonconformists"—poets and ballad singers—were not regarded as such in the Okefinokee community. Poets like William Tennyson Chesser and Hamp Mizell stood not at the fringe but at the center of Okefinokee society. They were respected as productive farmers, crafty hunters, skilled fishermen, and wise counselors. These individuals may have been considered exemplary because they had achieved that vital balance between the inner and the outer self. Strangers to the area have been known to call these people "eccentric." As Uncle Lone Thrift, keeper of the boats at Suwannee Lake, used to say: "I'm peculiar to the average man." To his way of thinking, the "average man" was so caught up in the materialistic goals of modern life that he had no place for quiet moments of contemplation. Uncle Lone was proud to be called "peculiar" or "stubborn." He liked to say that "a man works and lives up to his talent. . . . Call me just anything."

Uncle Jack Mizell would call most of the older swampers "light'ood knot Georgia Crackers." It was a special, appropriate name. Uncle Jack's superlative adjective was "light'ood knot." He used it the way a lyricist repeats his favorite metaphor. A heavy rainfall was a "freshet," and a very heavy one a "master freshet." But the heaviest downpour he could remember was nothing less than a "light'ood knot floater." Uncle Jack used to play the fiddle for square dances. He also "called the sets" on occasion. Sometimes when the mood was "just right," he did not tell the gents to "grab your pardners"; no, he instructed them to "fetch your light'ood knots."

What is a "light'ood knot"? It is an almost impenetrable mass of fat pine, "lightwood." Heavy with resin, it makes an excellent torch as well as kindling for starting fires. This is the very last part of the pine tree to fall victim to decay or destruction. In many ways Uncle Jack summed up the enduring character of these proud people with his own special metaphor. He declared he was among the last of the "light'ood knot Georgia Crackers," and he was probably right.

THE WAY TO

BILLYS ISLAND

*Francis Harper's account of his first journey
to the heart of the swamp*

THE WAY TO BILLYS ISLAND

The river St. Mary has its source from a vast lake, or marsh, called Ouaquaphenogaw, which lies between Flint and Oakmulge rivers, and occupies a space of near three hundred miles in circuit. This vast accumulation of waters, in the wet season, appears as a lake, and contains some large islands or knolls, of rich high land; one of which the present generation of Creeks represent to be a most blissful spot of the earth: they say it is inhabited by a peculiar race of Indians, whose women are incomparably beautiful; they also tell you, that this terrestrial paradise has been seen by some of their enterprising hunters, when in pursuit of game, who being lost in inextricable swamps and bogs, and on the point of perishing, were unexpectedly relieved by a company of beautiful women, whom they call daughters of the sun, who kindly gave them such provisions as they had with them, which were chiefly fruit, oranges, dates, &c. and some corn cakes, and then enjoined them to fly for safety to their own country; for that their husbands were fierce men, and cruel to strangers: they further say, that these hunters had a view of their settlements, situated on the elevated banks of an island, or promontory, in a beautiful lake; but that in their endeavors to approach it, it seemed to fly before them, alternately appearing and disappearing. They resolved, at length, to leave the delusive pursuit, and to return; which, after a number of inexpressible difficulties, they effected. When they reported their adventures to their countrymen, their young warriors were enflamed with an irresistible desire to invade, and make a conquest of, so charming a country; but all their attempts have hitherto proved abortive, never having been able again to find that enchanting spot, nor even any road or pathway to it; yet they say that they frequently meet with certain signs of its being inhabited, as the building of canoes, footsteps of men, &c.

These words from the celebrated "Travels" of William Bartram, the early American naturalist, embody the atmosphere of legendary mystery and superstition that enshrouded the Okefinokee Swamp as recently as a century ago. There are legends of the place to this very day. Without a doubt this great natural feature of southeastern Georgia is rich in historical and literary associations. Chronicles of the Indian wars, historical works from colonial times, United States Senate documents, state reports of Georgia, stories of Confederate deserters, tales of fiction, Maurice Thompson's essays—all these and more have contributed to the enduring fame of the Okefinokee. In 1885 Thompson fittingly described it as "one of those great gloomy swamps . . . in southeastern Georgia, so repellent and yet so fascinating, so full of interest to the naturalist, and yet so little explored." Though parts of the Okefinokee have been visited by a few men of scientific interests within the last fifty years, and by hunters for a much longer period, it has remained for many a virtual *terra incognita*—a place of haunting mystery and fancied terrors.

Thus it was with no slight feeling of exhilaration that I found myself, early on a morning in May 1912, in a little party approaching the northern borders of the great swamp. A kindly Cracker who escorted us from the train station at Braganza the previous evening now greeted us with a mule and wagon to carry us through the open pine forest that encompasses the Okefinokee. But riding a wagon was not to be thought of on such a morning. A bright sky smiled upon us, and a gentle swamp breeze murmured in the tree tops. Unfamiliar bird voices constantly lured me ahead along the cart path or aside into the low undergrowth of saw palmetto. In the distance several bobwhites piped cheerily, and chimney swifts ("chimney sweepers," according to our host) circled on rapid wings above the trees. Bluebirds, purple martins, crested flycatchers, cardinals, flickers, a wood pewee, a brown-headed nuthatch, meadowlarks, and a mourning dove were but a few of the old acquaintances I was glad to see in this new environment.

The morning was less than half done when our six-mile wagon journey ended at Cowhouse Landing. The pines gave way abruptly at the water's edge to a belt of cypress, and the still depths of the great Okefinokee stretched before us.

In a cluster of young cypresses lay a boat of good proportions. Its bow rested high upon a log mooring; among the slender branches of the saplings stood the required paddles and pole sticks. But our faith in the craft received a rude shock when we launched it only to witness a gushing of swamp water through the bottom. Such was the occasion of our first glimpse into the resourcefulness of the swampers. Our guide taught us how to gather resin from the nearby pines by lancing and draining the delicate bark. Then he showed us how to boil the resin over a little fire of "light'ood knots." Soon the pitchy mass perfectly sealed the more conspicuous cracks, and the craft was swamp worthy.

The sun was near its zenith when we loaded the baggage with care and embarked. From his position in the bow our guide, Dave Lee, was stationed to guide us over the tortuous water trail. He began to lead us through unblazed cypress "bays" and wide expanses of "prairie" to his home on Billys Island, a trip of some eighteen miles. One of my companions stationed himself amidships where he could bail to the most advantage. From the stern I seconded, as best I could, Dave's masterful handling of paddle and pole.

Through a slight gap in the thickest portion of the tree belt which borders the mainland, our trail led by degrees into a region of open glades—the very fairest part of the Cowhouse Run. The run passed between lines of cypresses from which hung long festoons of Spanish moss, gently swaying in the breeze and half concealing the trunks of trees. Vistas were disclosed glade after glade, fringed on all sides by slender files of the cypress. The beauty was exquisite, almost supernatural. Every part of the opening, save the run, was occupied by the far-spreading sphagnum in which Dave pointed out many winding trails of otter and alligator. The luxuriant blades of "never-wet" (*Orontium aquaticum*) in the water almost shut out a view of the surface, and they rustled and scraped along the sides of the boat as Dave's vigorous poling drove it onward.

As we passed on our right a group of particularly tall slash pines, we pointed our boat's prow toward another pine that tow-

"The very fairest part of the Cowhouse Run." May 1912.

ered above the southern horizon. We were now on Mud Lake. Dave called these trees "saplin's" just as he called any pine of any size. The trees were his landmarks, and he apparently had made many journeys through this part of the swamp. Why were there no blazes or marks on the trees? Dave explained there was no need to make it easy for outsiders to find the trail through the inner reaches of the swamp. So the Billys Island people maintained a special proprietorship over these solitary places.

To Dave these places were perfectly familiar. Born and reared in the heart of the swamp, he had never traveled far or long beyond its borders. He had experienced very little contact with the complexities of civilization to have been spoiled thereby. At nineteen he was an experienced bear hunter, sturdy, resourceful, and well versed in the lore of the swamp. I shall never forget an incident which occurred before we had started our trip. We were exploring the headwaters of the Suwannee River, and I told Dave that he had surely heard Stephen Foster's "Suwannee River," thereupon bursting into a spontaneous rendition of a few familiar lines. In a moment he replied, "No sir. I never hain't hyearn that un." Such was the isolation of the swampers in the old days.

Dave seemed to know the name of every bird, animal, and plant in the swamp. And he spoke deliberately. He had learned carefully the lessons of nature's school. When we found the warm water of the prairie none too refreshing for a drink, Dave alone knew how to get good, cool water. He created a little whirlpool with his hand beside the boat and drew cool water from the depths of what he called a "'gator-hole."

Our afternoon's progress was enlivened by the sight of seven or eight white ibises far in our front. Naturally Dave was the first to see them. He called them by their swamp name, "curlews." In an orderly line above the cypresses they sped westward on strong and graceful wings.

In the late afternoon our boat emerged from a densely wooded portion of the run and glided forth upon the silent stretch of the "Big Water." Here it seems that a long aisle has been made in the cypress forest, through which the gentle current of the most gentle Okefinokee flows. Its shorelines are lined with "hoorah bush" and bay, and close behind rise the stately ranks of cypress. Its deep, dark waters shelter the jackfish, the bream, and the gamy bass; here, too, one may catch glimpses of the great saurian of the swamp whose manner, since he has become acquainted with the hunter's modern firearms, is far less fierce than his looks.

Our forked sticks, now useless, were laid aside. Dave took the stern seat with the single remaining paddle (for the other somehow had been lost); with well-directed strokes he urged the heavily-laden boat at a fair rate along the stream. Even from that position he pointed out to our unaccustomed eyes a dark, low-lying shape or two that crossed our course a hundred yards in front. The 'gators are as many feet in length, he said, as there are inches between eyes and nostrils; and since these are usually the only parts that are plainly visible above the surface, they offer a ready criterion of measurement. The Big Water appears to foster the growth of big 'gators, for those we saw could have been little less than twelve feet in length.

After we traveled several miles, the waterway again became obstructed with "bonnets" and other aquatic vegetation. With the aid of those trusty forked sticks, we passed through the Minne Lake Narrows, where Dave pointed out the former roosting places of egrets, white ibises, and water-turkeys. The lake itself, like Big Water, is simply a deeper and slightly wider part of the stream, and through this gloomy, canyonlike gap in the forest we hastened to the foot of the lake. Night was beginning to settle upon us.

Then, without a suggestion of warning, Dave commenced a weird, prolonged halloo—a sort of yodel, with measured cadences—that broke the stillness of the night and resounded afar over the swamp. We could scarcely suppress our amazement, but we listened while he gave once or twice again those remarkable notes. Since Dave did not volunteer an explanation, we felt it would be best to leave the subject unmentioned. In very truth, the mysteries of the Okefinokee had not all vanished. I learned later that we had just witnessed the "Billys Island yell," and it was a signal to the folks on Billys Island that Dave and his party were safely headed home. The astonishing circumstance here is the tremendous distance—a beeline of some two miles—Dave's yell had traveled.

Cutting through the darkness, we were confronted by an immense cypress bay whose dense gloom added greatly to the difficulties of the obscure and crooked run. For anyone except a native, who knew by heart every rod of the way, it would have been folly to attempt a nocturnal trip over the remaining distance to Billys Lake and Billys Island. But Dave was master of the situation. Taking position in the bow again, he cast the rays of our bull's-eye lantern from side to side while seeking out the right openings in the tangled undergrowth. In many a place where the run became too confined for the free use of the paddle, we grasped a cypress knee or an overhanging

Jackson Lee's home on Billys Island. Tradition has it that the island was named for Billy Bowlegs, a Seminole chieftain who made camp here in the 1820s. May 1912.

limb, and by pushing or pulling forged slowly ahead.

When the bushes scraped our faces or tugged at our hats, it was a trifle disquieting to recall the many snakes that we had heard during the day as they dropped into the water from their resting-places along the branches projecting over the run. Another barred owl challenged our intrusion into its "ancient, solitary reign" by sending forth its cry from a cypress above us, and it responded to our imitative calls from a still nearer perch. Thus, for three extraordinarily long, wearisome hours, during which our boat more than once wandered off the trail, we struggled through the swampy tangle, finally to emerge into a bonnet-covered lagoon under a starlit sky. In another minute we had gained the open water of Billys Lake, and with lighter hearts we turned our course eastward.

So it was in the middle of the night, after nearly twelve hours of continuous poling and paddling, that we finally made the landing of Billys Island. The heart of the great Okefinokee at last! We trudged up through the cornfield to Dave's home. Deep-throated bearhounds greeted us, and Dave sort of introduced us to them before he went indoors. Soon his mother and sister appeared from the sleeping quarters and crossed the breezeway into the kitchen. Despite our protests, they set out food and drink for our refreshment. So true to tradition is southern hospitality, even in a wilderness home of logs.

Holding a blazing pine knot in one hand, Dave then led the way to the single upper room which formed a sleeping apartment. I tell you, no feathery couch in the thronged communities of men could have been half so welcome as this mattress of straw on a homemade bed. What a relief for our worn-out limbs this bed was.

Before going to sleep, we chatted briefly with two fellow occupants of the loft: Dave's older brother, Bryant, and their pal, "Gator Joe" Saunders. Understandably they were curious about the intentions of the first naturalist they had ever seen—or possibly even heard of. I am not sure if my words satisfied them, but all of us soon were sound asleep.

Morning presented an extraordinary pleasure. We observed unobtrusively the manner of life of the only human inhabitants of the remote interior of the Okefinokee. I felt that the lives of these sober, self-reliant people reflected the true freedom of the wilderness, no less than its solitude and privations. Some half a century earlier, perhaps, the father and mother had established a home on Billys Island. They and the ever-increasing members of the second and third generations had continued to draw a livelihood from the manifold resources of the swamp. The longleaf pines furnished the timbers of their dwelling; the sandy loam of the clearing produced their annual supply of corn, sweet potatoes, and several smaller crops such as "pinders" (peanuts) and sugar cane; in the surrounding woods their cattle and razor-backed hogs found sustenance.

But no small part of their daily fare was derived from the wildlife around them. Deer, raccoons, opossums, rabbits, and squirrels (and of two kinds!), fish, soft-shelled "cooters" (turtles), wild turkeys, bobwhites, and many of the larger water birds—all these were secured for the table whenever opportunity offered. The bears, whose depredations in some years prevented a suitable increase in the drove of razor-backs, were hunted with hounds and made to compensate with their own flesh for any deficiency in the supply of home-cured bacon. Not only did the family enjoy the

The hunters camped on broom-sedge at the edge of a cultivated field. Skulls of bear, wildcat, and raccoon are trophies of earlier hunts. Left to right: David Lee, Farley Lee, Lem Lee, Francis Harper, and "Gator" Joe Saunders. May 1912.

product of the tame bees that swarmed in upright sections of hollow cypress logs about the yard, but the young men gathered probably an even greater store of wild honey from the "bee-gums" in the swamp. They marketed the skins of the alligator, bear, raccoon, wildcat, and otter, and obtained in trade the few necessities of life which the Okefinokee itself did not furnish them.

Bryant and Joe evidently had been preparing for a 'gator hunt on Honey Island Prairie, and this morning they set out. They were taking with them a boat for navigating the watery prairie and were transporting it over the four-mile length of Billys Island by means of horse and wagon. They had also converted some short sections of round pine logs into a set of cart wheels for hauling the boat across the width of Honey Island. As usual on their journeyings to various parts of the swamp, they were accompanied by a couple of redoubtable bearhounds.

The very next day the 'gator hunters surprised us by turning up again on Billys Island. "I thought you were goin' ter be gone two weeks," I remarked to Bryant. "We would 'a' been, if we hadn' had such bad luck," he replied, and then unfolded the story. They both had been harnessed up to the boat in pulling it on wheels over the watery pineland of Honey Island, when their dogs started a bear. The latter, unaware of the whereabouts of the men, almost ran them down as they fled before the dogs. Bryant quickly unharnessed himself and made for his gun in the boat. But Joe panicked without taking time to unharness himself, and tore off through the woods at such a rate that when the boat bumped into a pine, its whole bow was practically demolished. Meanwhile the bear passed right by them. The mishap forced

them to return to Billys Island for tools and material to rebuild the boat.

When the hunters were ready to go back to Honey Island three days later, Wood and I took advantage of the opportunity to enlarge our acquaintance with the swamp by accompanying them. Before proceeding half a mile southward on Billys Island, Joe spied a six-foot 'gator in a small pond, sneaked up, and fired a load of buckshot at it. The 'gator sank out of sight, but after Joe had given the "'gator grunt"—"*umph, umph*"—several times, it rose twice more and exposed itself to further shots. Joe then walked around to the other side of the pond and detected the reptile lying on the bottom. Shortly they pulled it out and skinned it in a matter of minutes. The hunters showed me the animal's musk glands and their openings on the lower jaw. The horny upper parts of the skin were left behind as unmarketable.

Farther on the hound called "Rattler" treed something, and we came up to him at a hollow cypress in a swampy area. Meanwhile the hound had crawled into a very small hollow and got stuck or "hung." It was quite a job to get the poor dog out. Then came the coon which yielded to the smoke caused by a small fire made at the end of the hollow; actually he walked out in a surprisingly deliberate manner. We held the dogs back a little, but in a minute they chased the quarry into a hollow stump. There Bryant grabbed it by the tail and held it on the stump while we took a look at it.

Immediately there began a hard tussle through a mile-wide bog lying between Billys and Honey islands, which goes by the somewhat misleading name of "strand" (Webster notes it is the "obsolete or Scotch and dialectical English" meaning "channel"). It soon became so deep that the

"The 'gator sank out of sight, but after Joe had given the 'gator grunt' — 'umph, umph' — several times, it rose twice more and exposed itself to further shots." May 1912.

The 'gator hunters and the day's catch. May 1912.

bearhounds with us half waded and half swam. After we had left the water lilies of the open water and entered an immense, swampy thicket, we frequently sank almost waist-deep into the holes of the uneven, root-entangled trail, or tottered here and there across a quivering bed of floating sphagnum.

"I reckon you fellers are findin' it pretty worrisome through hyere," remarked Bryant. After consuming more than an hour in our passage through the "strand," we emerged gradually upon the *terra firma* of Honey Island. Here a hunting shanty, set amid the straight lofty trunks of the long-leaf pines, became a temporary abode. An Indian mound before it reminded us of the aboriginal inhabitants who once pursued the deer in the surrounding forest. The smoke of our campfire drifted freely into the open doorway and through the wide spaces between the smooth pine logs that formed the walls of the cabin. The roof was more compactly built, and its roughhewn shingles interposed a welcomed barrier between us and the rain. A small platform in the interior served for sleeping quarters.

One of the hounds, which four days earlier had chased a bear and disappeared into the swamp, was awaiting the 'gator hunters at the hunting shanty. It had been without food for four days, except for what it may have been able to capture by its own efforts, and the reunion of dog and master was a glad one.

Soon my three camp mates were off for the northeastern end of the island where they flushed four sandhill cranes and jumped a deer in the edge of a pond. Just as darkness settled in, I returned to camp. Then I heard more of that strange music which always startles me—swamp hollering. I was unversed in the unwritten rules of the matter, and I assumed my friends at the upper end of the island were having fun. Expecting to meet them on the way home, I started out toward them. Soon all of us were together again around our friendly campfire.

Gator Joe asked me somewhat impatiently if I had heard them holler, and if so, why I hadn't answered. "When you hyear anybody hollerin', you holler back," he said with undisguised sternness. Clearly he was concerned about my getting lost or being harmed. And so Joe taught me rule one about the art of hollering. Even if I had been aware of what was required, I was then—and am yet—totally incapable of producing a sound at all akin to the marvelous swamp yodeling. Of course I could have made some loud noise, but it would have been a virtual desecration in an atmosphere that had been reverberating with the exquisite music made by two masters, Gator Joe Saunders and Bryant Lee.

During these days the sun shone brightly and the nights were clear and bright with stars. While sitting around the campfire that evening, it was quite natural that Wood and I, under the influence of the spectacle overhead, should happen to touch upon such astronomical subjects as the revolving earth, its shape, and its relation to the sun and moon.

Astounding as it may seem, Joe and Bryant apparently had *never even heard* that the earth is round! More discussion about its shape left Joe quite unconvinced. "No sirree-man-bob, you cain't make me believe that. Whut do you think erbout it, Bryant?" The question brought a prompt response: "Well, Joe, hit 'pyears ter me erbout like hit do ter you." I contended that during the night we would reach a position about where China was at the moment, on the underside of the earth; this left them particularly unresponsive. Finally as we prepared for sleep, we went to our quarters—three of us inside the small shanty, and Joe with his big frame in the little boat near the water. Momentarily Joe ended the discussion about astronomy with his last words of the evening: "Well, boys, I guess I better fasten muh boat ter the shanty ternight, so it won't drop off when we git down ter where China is!"

The next evening (May 15) was a good one for a novel pastime called "striking." The shallow water bordering Billys Island is perfect for it. We waded slowly about in a stooping position, holding a bundle of blazing light'ood knots in the left hand and a machete in the right hand. When a fish of sufficient size was sighted, one of us would make a swift downward stroke and cut the booty in two. Jackson's eight-year-old son Marion eagerly followed us and strung the captured fish on a stick. In recent years I think not so much of our meager catch (a small jackfish and a perch or two) but of the vivid scene—the tense, stooping figures and the flaring torches lighting up the trunks of the pines against the inky blackness of the night.

The greater part of the next two days was spent in reconnoitering the wide expanse of Chase Prairie, especially the northeastern

With blazing pine torches and homemade machetes, the fishermen moved stealthily through the shallow water, poised to "strike." May 1912.

portion. The prairie itself possessed a won-drous fascination. I thought of three very important persons in my life: my preceptor, Lane Cooper; the great American natural-ist, William Bartram; and the English poet Wordsworth. It was Cooper who first sug-gested that some lines in Wordsworth's "Ruth" must have been inspired by Bartram:

The youth of green savannahs spake,
And many an endless, endless lake,
With all its fairy crowds
Of islands, that together lie
As quietly as spots of sky
Among the evening clouds.

The impressive scenery of Chase Prairie has a charm which surpasses that of any other Okefinokee prairie that I have seen. The view was more than ample reward for the day's excursion. Hoping to capture per-manently what I keenly felt, I put on some climbing irons and ascended a slash pine on one of the prairie heads. I must have climbed to a height of fifty feet or so where I took several photographs of the enchant-ing watery expanse before me.

After nightfall we paddled southward along the canal for a couple of miles, hop-ing to secure a photograph of a big 'gator by flashlight. We caught the glint from a big one's eyes and by degrees came quite close to it. Noting that it might be a twelve-footer, Dave put the boat a little too far to one side, and before I could set off the flash powder (a cumbersome exercise, one can imagine), the animal sank out of sight.

While the rest of us slept peacefully on the morning of May 18, Dave took his boat up the north fork of the canal. He noted the fresh trail of a bear engaged in digging up the eggs of turtles (probably the Florida terrapin, *Pseudemys floridana*) which had been laid in the banks of the canal. He said the bear almost attacked him, but the mammal seemed more interested in fleeing than in fighting.

In the afternoon we began our trip back to Billys Island. While we were poling down a quiet fork of the swamp, a wild, sweet chant broke upon our ears: *swee-swee-swee-swee, swee-swee* (the last two notes at a lower pitch). I was bound to add a new warbler to the swamp list, I thought as I stepped ashore in the tangled thicket on the bank. I waited a bit for the bird to ap-pear. Then I hit upon the expedient of imitating the song. It worked like a charm. The bird flew in my direction as each of us responded to the other. The sight I beheld nearly took my breath: not the hooded war-bler, as I had expected, but a bird with dull brown upper parts, a light stripe over the eye, and yellowish underparts. A Swain-son's warbler! In silence we gazed upon each other for several minutes. Then the bird began beckoning its supposed rival and grew excited. Shortly he grew impatient and flew off.

The next day, May 19, gave me the plea-sure of photographing Dave's folks in their comfortable log-built home. I also strolled southward on the island to a cypress pond and photographed a pair of prothonotary warblers at their nest in a stump.

The *rara avis* of the Okefinokee, of course, is the ivory-billed woodpecker. At that time a few pairs still survived on the remote and well-nigh inaccessible Minnies Lake Islands lying in the depths of the swamp several miles north of Billys Lake. On May 20 Dave and I set out for the trea-sure. As we pushed through a difficult run toward the islands, I told Dave about the tragic fate of the great auk and the pas-

"Cypress heads" and water lilies on scenic Chase Prairie. May 1912.

senger pigeon. After a day's disheartening struggle through labyrinthine ways, we discovered that we were absolutely no nearer our destination than we were when we started. Thus my initial quest for the elusive ivorybill ended. (I might add that fortune smiled at me from around the corner, so to speak, in December 1916. I heard what the ornithologist Chapman noted in his handbook as "the note of a penny trumpet," and I guessed I was in the presence of this nearly extinct bird. The next day Farley and Dave, who had been absent when I heard the sound, confirmed that it surely came from the ivorybill. Later I would hear Arthur Allen's faithful sound-recording of the bird and would know for sure that the bird at Dinner Pond Lake was authentic indeed. It was within a year that Sam Mizell shot one at Cravens Hammock

and sent it to the Academy of Natural Sciences of Philadelphia.)

May 21 found Dave and me returning to the northern border of the swamp. My delightful sojourn was coming to an end. We pitched our tent beneath a thick stand of magnolias and live oaks. The ground was covered by an immensely thick carpet of fallen magnolia leaves. The next day we poled over the shallow water and deep muck of Floyds Island Prairie. Before dark we made it to Big Water, where we pitched camp at a "hunter's camp"—a mere platform of logs "on top of the swamp." While we prepared for supper, we were serenaded by a savage symphony provided by two great alligators of the Big Water. Thereafter it was not difficult for me to comprehend how Bartram could write: "The earth trembles with his thunder. . . . The shores and

The Lees of Billys Island. May 1912.

· 48 ·

forests resound his dreadful roar." Aside from the huge reptiles' generally tolerant attitude toward man, there was nothing to prevent them from pulling us off the platform during the hours of darkness and leaving our bodies on the bottom of Big Water to soften up a bit for later consumption.

Soon we passed through Dinner Pond Lake again. (What a curious and yet euphonious name!) At last we gained solid ground at Cowhouse Landing, and we left behind the glories of the Okefinokee. My life would never again be the same. Indeed, whoever has beheld the manifold charms of this paradise of woods and waters, must come away fascinated and spellbound. Its majestic pines and cypresses, its peaceful waterways and lily-strewn prairies, together with the wild creatures that inhabit them, should have been safeguarded forever from the lumberman's despoiling operations.

It was during a meditation such as this that Dave spoke to me an absolutely puzzling and fascinating arrangement of words:

"Ol' Young was a-slippin' in a run, to shoot a fat Po' Jo settin' on a dead live-oak."

"Where did you learn that, Dave?" I asked.

"My mother" (Mrs. Nancy Lee).

What a clever juxtaposition of words of different and opposite meanings! Was this the first time I felt the people of the swamp possessed a charm and dignity worthy of preserving? If so, I had not yet realized what an extraordinary wealth of folklore was also here. I did not make a systematic effort to gather folk material immediately, but within a decade collecting Okefinokee lore had become my primary objective as I returned to the swamp again and again.

The cautious reserve of the Okefinokee folk slowly but surely melted away in the warmth of genuine mutual friendship. Before long they took delight in generously sharing their enjoyment of simple cultural pastimes with those who, coming from far away, deeply appreciated the privilege of recording and so preserving their contributions to folk literature and music.

OKEFINOKEE

SAMPLER

---

*A miscellany compiled by Delma E. Presley from
the papers of Francis Harper*

HAMP MIZELL · 1884–1948

He was a superlative friend—genial, warm-hearted, and generous to an extraordinary degree. Our friendship, established on my first trip in 1912, continued unabated as long as he lived. Despite having a full measure of human trials and tribulations, he was a good-natured man. At one time during the Great Depression, he offered to

Hamp Mizell, troubador of the Okefinokee. May 1930.

share his modest resources with me. He knew I was tied down by a somewhat uncongenial means of livelihood and would have liked to exchange it for a more tranquil existence in a more natural environment.

To Hamp I owe a special tribute for the abundance and variety of folk material that fills these pages—hunting adventures; stories of his friends, neighbors, and relatives; folk songs; fiddle tunes; banjo pieces; hollering—and for the opportunity to know his friends. Some of his older friends, such as Lone and Owen Thrift, Zeke Henderson, and J. D. Hendrix, shared marvelous tales of bygone days in and around the swamp. The insights they provided into those days are altogether priceless.

My older brother, Roland, had known Hamp since August 1902, when he had joined P. L. Ricker of the Bureau of Plant Industry in Washington for the first botanical reconnaissance of the Okefinokee swamp. On that occasion they had secured the services of Hamp's older brother, Sam Mizell. Sam guided them for a few days along the Suwannee Canal as far as the enchanting Chase Prairie, taking a side trip to Bugaboo Island.

At the turn of the century the Mizell homestead, close to the eastern border of the swamp and several miles north of Camp Cornelia, was presided over by Josiah Mizell. Eldest son of William Mizell, Josiah had moved from Camden County to Charlton County as a young boy. He had served as a member of the "Okefinokee Rifles" of the Confederate Army, and in 1866 he married Martha Johns. Official records show eight children in the Mizell household: John D., Sam, and Hamp, Amanda, Eliza, Emily, Florence, and Rhoda. Hamp was the youngest. The crops of their farm doubtless included corn, sweet potatoes,

sugar cane, cowpeas, tomatoes, watermelons, and other regional staples, together with the resources of the adjacent swamp and its borderlands; deer, ducks, sandhill cranes, wild turkeys, bobwhites, and a fine variety of food fishes provided them with an ample diet. They received a sufficient cash revenue from the sale of alligator hides and furs of the bear, raccoon, skunk, and otter.

Hamp told Alexander S. McQueen that "Josiah Mizell never moved from his original homestead; never swapped horses; never was arrested; never had a case in court; and reared a family of eight children and never had a doctor in his home until all his children were grown."

Some income was provided by the sale of lumber and turpentine. Altogether, the life of the Mizells and their neighbors was simple, wholesome, and satisfying. They had sufficient leisure to cultivate vocal and instrumental music, dancing and storytelling, to attend religious services, and to perform neighborly deeds of kindness.

I first met Hamp on the streets of Waycross, Georgia, on May 4, 1912. Little did I then realize what a wonderful friend he would become. He provided me with a far greater amount of folklore than any of my other swamp friends. In those times he had an unbounded enthusiasm for imparting all sorts of folk material—prose and verse, vocal and instrumental. It was Hamp Mizell to whom Alexander S. McQueen turned for "insider's information" about the swamp when he was writing the *History of the Okefenokee Swamp* (1926). Hamp was so resourceful that Mr. McQueen named him as coauthor. In his *History of Charlton County* (1932), Mr. McQueen wrote that Hamp was "the one man who probably knows more about the Okefenokee swamp, the nature and habits of its birds and animals, than any man living."

From the start he contributed to my knowledge. He said that his brother, Sam, had worked with him as assistant to John M. Hopkins, the surveyor of the immense timber lands in the swamp for the Hebard Company. Among the important elements of the fauna he mentioned were ivory-billed woodpeckers, pileated woodpeckers (or "good-god woodpeckers"), egrets, wood ibises (or "baldheads, 'cause they have heads so bare you could write on 'em with a pencil or scratch 'em with a knife"), sandhill cranes, great blue herons, wild turkeys, alligators, and *two kinds* of bears (hog bear of 300–400 pounds and Seneca bear of 500–600 pounds, having a "white throat

patch"). One can imagine how this partial account whetted my desire to see with my own eyes the wonders of the Okefinokee animal life.

After a sojourn of several months in the swamp in 1921, I set out northward on August 24 via the lumber railroad from Billys Island. I spent most of the day at the small settlement of Hopkins (some six miles from the small village of Manor), where Hamp took me to see his father-in-law, James D. Hendrix. Mr. Hendrix shared some interesting faunal notes, including the observation that there are "a right smart" [a plentiful number] of fox squirrels. Before the afternoon was over, Hamp posed for a scene that truly represented a camp in the piney woods. The essential items are all there: the tent, his deer-catching dog named "Brown," mounted deer heads, a gun, and a hunting horn made by his father, Josiah.

Almost a year later I was with a party of biologists which had a stop-over for several hours at Hopkins. Friendly Hamp took advantage of the occasion and introduced us to remote areas of Suwannee Lake which he was developing into an extremely attractive and productive fishing area. The man in charge of the boats, an unusual fellow named Lone Thrift, was half poet and half philosopher. Uncle Lone provided us with ample paddles and boats; thus began a long series of visits to this spot where such a quaint character held court for me and others, off and on, for the next twenty years.

Between 1922 and 1929 I did not visit the swamp. This seven years was the longest interval between my visits from 1912 through 1944. To make up for the precious time lost, I made annual trips for the next eleven years. By the time I arrived in 1929, Hamp and Uncle Lone had seen the Okefinokee stories (largely from the eastern and central parts of the swamp) that I had published in 1926 and 1927. [The publications alluded to are probably "Tales of the Okefinokee," *American Speech*, vol. 1 (1926), pp. 407–20, and "The Mammals of the Okefinokee Swamp Region of Georgia," *Proceedings of the Boston Society of Natural History*, vol. 28 (1927), pp. 191–396.] These apparently inspired them to offer whatever contributions they could make to our common cause. And what a wonderful harvest it was! In the past I had been able to spend only brief, tantalizing visits of not more than several hours with Hamp. In late July of 1929, however, I had six glorious days

with him at Suwannee Lake. Each day was an almost continual round of bird notes, frog photographs, folk-songs, banjo and fiddle pieces, stories about the people and the wildlife of the Okefinokee. Also there was the personal good fortune of seeing an alligator bellow for the first time. I got to know Uncle Lone Thrift better as well as Owen Thrift, who lived several miles northeast of Suwannee Lake.

In August 1931 I had the pleasure of attending an old-fashioned "frolic" of some twenty-five people who had gathered on the

"*Hamp posed for a scene which truly represented a camp in the piney woods. The essential items are all there: the tent, his deer-catching dog named 'Brown,' mounted deer heads, a gun, and a hunting horn made by his father, Josiah.*" *August 1921.*

greensward beside Hamp Mizell's home. Knowing that I would like to make a film of the occasion, Hamp arranged a daytime performance in the open to facilitate my work with the still and motion-picture cameras. As Hamp shouted to all, this was indeed "a happy time in Georgia!"

"Doc" Dorminy brought his fiddle, and Ed Strickland (of Waycross) showed up with a banjo. Hamp "beat the strings" on the doctor's fiddle. Big Will Cox, besides acting as the caller (a dandy one, too), took part in the dancing. Luke Thrift, Lonnie Thrift, Lester Barber, Maggie Mizell (Hamp's wife), Bertie Thrift, Ella Thrift, Mamie Roberson, and Olive Pitman all took part too. The men wore regular work clothes (overalls in three cases), while the girls were more or less dressed up and furnished a lot of color. A fair crowd of onlookers consisted mostly of women and children, some of them sitting on a pile of lumber in the shade of several pines.

Old-fashioned square dancing or frolics seem to have been held all through the Okefinokee region as far back as any one can remember. They are said to have flourished particularly among the younger folk of the "Hardshell" or Primitive Baptist communities. These dances go by the name of "breakdown," not "Virginia reel," a term heard locally only a few decades ago.

Harrison Lee recalled frolics on Billys Island in the old days that commenced in late afternoon and continued all night 'till about ten o'clock the next morning, with

The Okefinokee folk gathered for a frolic at Hamp Mizell's place in the summer of 1931. Fiddler Doc Dorminy is on the far left.

the table set all that time. Mattie Chesser, of Chessers Island, said that at Irvin Privat's place (probably in Charlton County) they would dance from sunset to sunrise and likewise keep the table set continuously.

For years Hamp Mizell was in special demand as master of ceremonies at such frolics, and he delighted in contributing to the festivities with banjo, fiddle, and voice. In this way he had become a veritable storehouse of information on the old songs and traditions; and it was very largely through the interest and zeal of Hamp and his cousin, Jack Mizell, that my collection of fiddle and banjo songs was secured. In singing them for me to copy down, Hamp often accompanied them with banjo or fiddle, meanwhile beating time on the floor or ground with one foot. He not only had preserved the songs and tunes of others but had contributed many of his own.

An old banjo at the Mizell place on the eastern border of the swamp was made by Hamp's brother John, with directions from their father. The grating was taken out of a sifter for meal, and a fawn skin was stretched over the rim. The fingerboard was whittled out of a black gum. The strings were made from threads twisted together and rubbed with beeswax so they would stick together. Several banjos about the swamp were similarly constructed. One was even made with a house cat's hide. It seems that a stray animal had appeared near a house on the Suwannee River, had been treed by the dogs, and had then met its fate at the hands of the owner of the place. The hide was removed and treated with potash to make the hair slip off; then it was placed on the banjo frame. Hamp claimed this particular instrument was one of the best he had ever played: "It had a ringing sound to it that I never heard in any other banjer."

Back to the frolic of 1931. Listen to Will Cox call the square dance at Hamp's place:

HANDS UP EIGHT

Hands up eight,
And move to the left
Halfway and promenade
Back with your pardner.

Swing your pardner
And swing your corner pardner
And promenade.

First couple out.
Lady round the gent.
Gent round the lady.
Meet in the center and swing.

Four hands around.
Ladies dose the doe.
Gents you know,
Swing your pardner.

First couple out
For the Iris trail.
Four hands around,
Swing your lady in the reel.

First couple out.
Lady to the right
And gent to the left.
Swing or cheat.

Three hands up
And shoot the 'gator.

First couple out.
Lady to the right, gent to the left.
Three hands up
And croquet walk.

Ladies to the center
And face to the wall.
Gents dance around 'em all.

Miss your pardner one time.
Miss your pardner two times.

Miss your pardner three times.
Swing 'er and promenade.

Ladies to the center
And right hand across.
Circle halfway and back
And don't forget your pardner
(or "light'ood knot" or "coon dog")

Drop one back.
Drop two back.
Drop three back.
Swing 'er and promenade.

Three hands up.
Bird in the cage.
Bird swing out, crow swing in.
On to the right an' going again.

I have the impression that the last two verses could be repeated endlessly, as the dancers engaged in what I recall as the "outside pick-up." The form of the square dance is familiar to most Americans. Some of the local lyrics are fascinating, however. The almost universal "shoot the star" has been replaced in the swampland by "shoot the 'gator." I asked Will and Hamp what "Ladies dose the doe" meant in verse four. "Just words," Hamp replied. Will agreed. Originally the French words for "back to back" (*dos à dos*) were understood, perhaps. But the meaning was lost on the swampers who, nevertheless, knew what to do when they heard "dose the doe."

Hamp and I were picking figs one afternoon at Uncle Owen Thrift's place when he taught me a number of fiddle songs. The fig tree was near the mud-and-stick chimney of Uncle Owen's house. I startled Hamp, perhaps, when I burst into a song my brother, Roland, had learned at the University of Georgia more than thirty years earlier:

I wish I had a load of poles
For to build my chimley higher.
For ev'ry time it rain an' hail,
It put out all my fire.

Hamp responded quickly with his local version:

I wish I had a load of sticks
To build my chimley higher,
Just to keep my neighbor's cats
From fallin' in my fire.

Enjoying himself, he offered another:

Last year was not a good crop year
For okra and corn, but for potaters.
Daddy didn' make no okra and corn,
But O Lord God, the taters.

"That come from right up hyere around Hoboken" (in Brantley County). "Old man Alonzo Dowling sang it. Probably made it up."

We were driving back to Hamp's place in his old Ford, and he told me about how Primitive Baptist meetings often would be combined with frolics, especially in the old days. Both events were designed to allow for a lot of social interaction. Hamp then recited one song the young people on Chessers Island used to sing. Sam and Allen Chesser were credited with the lyrics:

SAPSUCKER

See that Sapsucker on that pine—
Oh how I wish that gal was mine.
I got drunk an' away she fled,
An' ever since then my head's been red.

Set my hen in the fodder stack.
Come along a hawk an' he hit her on the back.
She flew off an' cack-cack-cack.
Her old bones went whickity-whack!

"Catfish" is popular in the swamp region. As Hamp said, "If a man can't play 'Catfish,' he ain't no banjer picker." A peculiar word in the song is "snout," so I asked what it meant: "Smellers," he said, "but we call 'em snouts (i.e., barbels)." The second and third stanzas were once heard in the Appalachian mountain states, but the first and final ones are pure Okefinokee.

CATFISH

See the catfish swim down the stream
Mouth full of butter an' his gill full of cream.
Caught the catfish by the snout,
And I throwed that catfish all about.

If you want to go courtin',
I tell you where to go.
Way down the country,
And way down below.

When you get there,
The ol' folks ain't home.
The gals all mad
And their heads not combed.

Jaybird settin' on a hickory limb.
He winked at me an' I at him.
Picked up a rock an' hit him on the shin.
Says he, by golly, don't you do that again.

The annual meeting of the Primitive Baptist churches of the Alapaha Association is one of the highlights of the year in the lives of the Okefinokee folk. On May 11, 1930 I was privileged to join Hamp and his family for this impressive occasion. I was touched to observe their sincere communion of bread and real wine and their "foot washing" which came after communion. At the end of the service, they held a "going hands around." As was the custom in old pioneer days, the members at the meeting might have been from churches far removed from each other. But all were brothers and sisters as they sang without musical accompaniment the final hymn. Men, some still singing, began shaking hands with the rest. Women and non-members joined in the occasion, and even I felt free to participate. Uncle Jesse Aldridge, preacher for the day, was a leader in the processional which allowed each member to shake each person's hand. Both men and women dabbed their eyes with handkerchiefs to express their sorrow upon leaving old friends. One gets the distinct impression that religious observances of the good Primitive Baptists are a more fundamental part of the lives of the Okefinokee folk than with the average citizens.

After returning from church, Hamp and I sat on the front porch and talked about local matters. For years I had been fond of a ballad Hamp knew by the title of "The Piney Woods Boys." But my favorite version had a setting in the swamp. Hamp called it Mary Hickox Lee's song, and it is probably true that the Lees of Billys Island are responsible for it.

THE BILLYS ISLAND BOYS

Come all you North Carolina girls
And listen to my noise,
If you want to be courted
By all the Billys Island boys.

And if you do,
Your portion will be,
Johnny Cake an' venison
Is all you'll see.

And when he goes a-courtin',
He'll drag him up a chair,
The first word he says is,
"Daddy killed a deer."

And the next word he says,
Before he sits down,

"Girls, ain't your johnny cake
Bakin' very brown?"

And when he goes to meeting,
You can tell him by his dress,
His ol' huntin' shirt,
And that's his very best.

His ol' sock legs,
And them ringed aroun',
And his ol' straw hat
More brim than crown

And when he gets you married
He'll put you on the hill,
And there he'll leave you
Against your will.

And then it's to leave
Or starve on the place.
And that's the way
Of the Billys Island race.

That Hamp knew songs from what he
called "slavery days" came as a surprise.
Like most rural counties of this region,
Charlton County was composed almost entirely of non-slaveholding yeoman farmers.
The county was formed in 1854 from the
inland portion of a "plantation county,"
Camden, whose eastern coastal border contains the rich lowlands that provided much
of Georgia's rice and cotton in antebellum
days. The original settlers of the Okefinokee had no firsthand knowledge of slavery,
but they were loyal to the Confederate
cause and many quickly enlisted. Were the
songs that follow brought back by those
who had served in the war?

RUN, NIGGER, RUN

See that nigger streak through the field.
The black snake catch him by the heel,
He run so far an' he run so fast
That he run slap through the hornet's nest.

Chorus:
Run, nigger, run, the patter-road'll catch you.
Run, nigger, run, it's almost day.

The dog he run an' the patter-road flew.
Why the devil can't a nigger run, too?
The nigger run an' the nigger flew.
The nigger tore his shirt in two.

(repeat chorus)

Hamp explained why the subject of the
song "tore his shirt in two": "He needed to
get faster." That fits the context of the
song, which actually invokes sympathy for
the fleeing slave. The term "patter-road"
probably is a corruption of "patroller," since
in plantation days in the old South, white
patrols were stationed at night with teams
of dogs for the purpose of catching runaway
slaves.

A brief, untitled piece also seems to take
the side of the black men and women who
had to work as industriously as bees for
their owners:

Big bee suck the punkin stem,
Little bee make the honey.
Niggers work in cotton an' corn,
An' the white folks tote the money.

Other songs from Hamp's repertoire of
music from Civil War days included "Blue
Tail Fly," "Uncle Ned," and "Cotton-eyed
Joe." One particularly enchanting piece was
called "My Dearest May." Hamp said that
his brother John's wife taught him the lyrics. The original singer might well have
been a black man. Hamp's voice contained
genuine sympathy as he recited.

MY DEAREST MAY

Old Massa give me a holiday,
An' I wish he'd give me more.

I'd go down by the riverside,
And row my boat from shore

Chorus:
O Lord, my dearest May.
You're lovely as the day.
Your eyes so bright,
They shine at night,
When the moon has gone away.

Then gently down the river
With a heart so light an' free,
To the cottage of my dearest May,
What I long so much to see.

(repeat chorus)

I listen to the waters,
As they so sweetly flow.
The coon among the branches play,
While the mink remains below.

(repeat chorus)

Hamp Mizell was one of those people who could play many roles and play them well. He was a hunter, fisherman, guide, and family man. But people always think of him as a musician—a ballad singer and maker. Had it not been for people like Hamp and the Chessers, music from the frontier probably would not have survived in the Okefinokee. The love of music was instinctive: "I've stuck the plough in the field many a time and run to the house to play a tune on the fiddle when it come to me," explained Hamp. "I reckon I've wrote out a thousand ballads for people, just to keep 'em a-goin'. If it wasn't for me—I don't want to brag—I reckon they'd a-died out."

Even though Hamp preferred to play and sing his favorite traditional fiddle and banjo pieces, I was able to convince him to share one of his own compositions. Like the troubadours before him, Hamp felt free to use words and phrases from other ballads and songs he had heard, providing the need arose. Folk music to Hamp was a living tradition, and he carried on that tradition in the manner of a carpenter who goes to his workshop or woodshed for basic materials to be fashioned into a new structure.

"A Day in Springtime" had been written on a piece of paper dated January 31, 1914. Hamp said he had gone before sunrise and sat on a log between Suwannee Lake and the Okefinokee, facing the "Big Head" on one side and the piney woods on the other. The words surely reflect an intimate, faithful picture of life on an Okefinokee farm, and they are based upon long experience and observation. Hamp recited the lines, and the orthography perhaps is more correct than it might have been had I copied the written verses.

A DAY IN SPRINGTIME

Think of a day in springtime,
When it's fair an' gray at dawn.
The sun comes up so welcome,
Then ev'rything is warm.

You see the birds so happy
Flyin' from tree to tree;
You see the flowers bloomin',
And hear the buzzin' bee.

The trees are flush an' buddin',
An' soon unfold their leaves.
We feel the air refreshin'
In ev'ry gentle breeze.

You see the farmer ploughing
An' stirring up the soil,
Getting ready for a crop another year
An' another six months' toil.

You hear his hens a-cackling,
His cows begin to low,
His horse sheds off his winter coat,
While up an' down the row

We see him plant his garden,
First of all the rest.
He plants it most in something
That the family thinks is best.

Then we see him later,
When the weather's gettin' warm.
He puts on his wide-rimmed hat
An' hoes around his corn.

Then we see the perspiration
Flowing from his brow.
We hear his wife a-callin',
"Dinner's ready now!"

Then he turns towards the house
With a slow an' easy walk.
He washes his face an' combs his hair
Before he eats or talks.

Hamp was an extraordinary storyteller. The tales that follow are only a few of many that he recollected over the years.

An Okefinokee "Jack-o-My-Lantern"

"It wasn't no moving light, but I'll tell you what it done. I'd been hunting with a chum of mine, and one of my dogs follered him when he went home. And a day or two later I went after him. Got on a horse and went in the night. In turning back, I saw something right aside the road. I thought it was a stump burning. It looked like a big ball of firecoal a-shining. But I knew there was no fire there when I went along, and it hadn't been long. It was right in front of an old house that had been standing there for years without anybody finishing building it. But when I got near enough, within about twenty-five feet of it, it just disappeared. I was intending to investigate it. I've always

made it a rule to investigate anything I seen. I don't believe in haints—don't believe in witchery."

The Lonesomest Thing You Ever Heard

"That's the lonesomest thing you ever heard in your life, of a dark night. A hog bear will bite a hog down an' slap 'im and drive 'im off in the swamp. An' him a-squealin' all the way an' beggin' for his life."

A Dog Runnin' Afoul of Alligators and a Bear

"One time my brother John and Nathan Dixon and Gad Roddenberry went out on the prairie back of our old place on a hunt. When it come evening, they eat supper in the boat, with a bucket of rations between 'em. Brother John got through first and took up the lantern an' strapped it to his head. And when he shined it around, there was a bear that had slipped up near 'em, no further than that well yonder. And when the light got on him, he growled. And brother John shot him and killed him. They hauled him into the boat an' rounded him up against a seat, lying there *thisaway* [as though the bear were asleep], till he got stiff.

"The next morning, when they come home, they put the 'gators they had killed in the end of the ditch my father had dug out in the prairie, so the sun wouldn't shine on 'em and spoil 'em.

"And when I came out on the logs through the bay to help 'em with the skinning, my ol' dog was there ahead of me. And when he come to the ditch, he

"No Shooting on or near this lake. No set (?) hooks. Do not pest the alagators" reads the sign at Hamp Mizell's fishing camp on Suwannee Lake in 1929.

thought the 'gators, with their bulk sticking out, were just some logs, and he walked out on them. 'Bout that time he noticed they was alligators, and jumped into the boat. And there he run into that bear kind of sittin' up. An' he lit out of there with all four legs stuck out sideways—like a flying squirrel—and him a-hollerin' for all he was worth. An' he went hitting the ground thataway for fifty yards, as you could tell by the trail, an' him a-yelpin' all the way!"

Two Kinds of Wolf in a Pit

"He was a preacher, and his name was Wolf. When he was a boy, he was a fiddler, and he got powerful drunk. He went out to lie down to get over a drunk, and he fell into a wolf pit. And a wolf was in it. He found the wolf was afraid of his playing the fiddle on one side, and the wolf was on the other."

A 'Gator at a Baptizing

"Ol' man Jim Hendrix said Wes T——— was a powerful scared man of an alligator. And he joined the church. When they went to baptize him, they took him down to a little lake in a creek. And old man Jim said whenever the preacher started leading

him into the water to start baptizing him, he could see Wes cutting his eye at every dark hole and under the bushes and all the corners around. He was looking for alligators all around. An' sure enough directly up popped a little one, about four foot long, right close. And old man Wes squalled out, 'Look at that damn 'gator!' He said that preacher looked at him for a *lonnng* time before he put his hands on him an' baptized him."

Cussin' Chickens in the Garden

"Ol man Jack ——— joined the church along about Wednesday. It was a big meetin' time—it just kept in motion, you know. It rocked on till about Friday, and there was a conference the next day. Some of the bretheren living close to Jack seen him out in the garden. The chickens had gotten in the garden an' was eating up his vegetables. And you see, he'd only been in the church from Wednesday to Saturday morning. And he got to frammin' after the chickens, just abusing and cussin' 'em, and this feller heard him. Ol' man Jack went to church that day. And they jerked him up for cussin' chickens in the garden! An' he told them if he'd knowed the '*damn chickens was goin' to get in the garden*,' he'd waited to next week to join."

LONE THRIFT · 1869–1951

He was born and raised on that large island at the end of our watery wilderness, the Cowhouse. His father had the reputation of being the kind of born leader who always draws a crowd around him. Uncle Lone said his father, Robert or "Uncle Bob," and his

friend Peter Griffin were known as bear fighters. "Not a bit afyeard of any bear in the world," Uncle Lone reminisced, "they would fight a bear with anything, if it was only a light'ood knot."

Lone lived on the Cowhouse until he was

twenty-three years old. He claimed his paternal great-grandfather came to this country from Ireland and quickly changed his name from "Flanigan or something" to Thrift. His grandfather, Carr Thrift (1805–1880), was born in Washington County, Georgia. Noticing that Uncle Lone signed his name "B. Thrift," I asked about the B. He explained that he had been called "Belonie" as a child, but the name was shortened—much to his approval—to "Lone." To every man, woman, and child in the swamp region, he was simply "Uncle Lone." They knew the name stood for the friend who was a skilled hunter, crafty fisherman, steady boatman, and sure carpenter.

He was in his fifty-third year when I first met him in 1921. Already he was established as the *genius loci* at Suwannee Lake, where he supervised boating and fishing activities. He had plenty of time to chat with friends and spin what he liked to call

Francis Harper called Lone Thrift the Saint Francis of the Okefinokee. June 1929.

"yarns" about life in the swamp. Some of his conversations were about religious matters—as he understood them. This man who knew nature best of all cared nothing about membership in any formal church or denomination, but he was deeply spiritual. In fact, over the years he had acquired a considerable reputation as a faith healer.

In a series of unplanned conversations on May 20, 1930 at Suwannee Lake, Uncle Lone and I talked freely and at random. I noticed among the flotilla of fishing boats at the lake one on which he had painted the name *Bew Dat*. When I ventured to ask the meaning, he explained that he gave it the name so that it would be like nothing else. Nothing had ever carried such a name, and he said it had no meaning beyond the fact that it was thoroughly original. He followed

with the observation that he, himself, was "a little bit different from the rest of the crowd—a little odd."

"Each feller has a trade of his own, if it's nothin' but loafin'," he later remarked, "Why sure. Now you are just as true to your work as I am to this lake, ain't you? A man works an' lives up to his talent." I replied that he might be using other words to describe the scientific attitude, "truth at all costs." "Truth at all costs, ain't that it?" he asked. "Truth'll win. It'll sure do that. Now, Mr. Harper, I'm peculiar to the average man. I've peculiar ideas about things." "Would people call you a conjure-doctor?" I asked. "Call me just anything," he replied. Soon he was earnestly relating the experiences that follow.

In the spring of 1930, Lone Thrift (left) *spent comfortable hours at Suwannee Lake telling the "yarns" Francis Harper* (right) *carefully transcribed.*

Hawks and the Power of Prayer

"This ain't a imaginary story. I'm goin' to tell you near 'bout just as it was. It was somewhere about nineteen hunderd an' three. I can't tell you exactly, but that'll cover it. At that time we lived in Wayne County—right side of a creek in a hammock, where the hawks was bad.

"Well, we had a little piece of land—about an acre—in front of the house. Had a new fence around it. When I started into the kitchen, one of the little boys was a-washin' behind me, to go to eat. He says, 'Yonder sets a hawk on the new-land fence now.' Well, I stopped and looked at it—saw him a-settin' there. I said, 'Don't bother him, son; he won't ketch 'em. I'm workin' on him, and don't let me forget it.'

"So after we ate, there come a good bunch a people. A lot of people visit my house—very much, wherever I live. They always done that. Well, my wife and the girls were washing up dishes from the breakfast. I and several others were setting out on the kitchen porch—had a little side porch to the kitchen. My wife stepped out there and said, 'The first time that ol' Uncle Johnny Wainwright' (that's the way she fetched it over) 'or ol' Uncle Eli Lee passes hyere, I expect them to take this wart off my finger.'

"I says, 'Let me see that wart.' She says, 'Oh, you can't do nothin',' and went to step into the kitchen. And she stepped by me, an' I catched my thumb over it just like that [rubbing his thumb over his forefinger]. She just stripped it out of my hand, because she knew I couldn't do anything.

"Well, I went to work. Left Sunday evening, you understand. In our yard there was big red oaks, limbs pretty close to the ground. Saturday night, when I came home from work, the same little boy that spoke to me about the hawk, he says to me as quick as I got home, 'Pa, Ma was a-feedin' the chickens last Wednesday morning, and the hawk struck among 'em right where she was feedin', an' missed, didn't get either of 'em. In a few minutes he was back, an' he struck again' (that's the rule of a hawk). 'And he caught one. And as he riz with it, that red oak jerked it out of his claws.'

"My wife was settin' there. She never said a word—never opened her mouth. I says, 'Son, he can't catch 'em. I'm working on him.' Well, I went back to work again of a Sunday evening, you understand.

"Well, when I came back Saturday night, my wife was unusually pleased about something—I didn't know what it was. You can tell when a woman's pleased about anything, can't you? After a while, we kept setting and talking, and the children a-playing. She says, 'You know, that wart's gone from my finger!' I says, 'No, I ain't looked for it.'

"Well, from then to now I get letters from time to time concerning of hawks—from people I never knew, too. I also have had people come to me for different things that come on to them, for different diseases. And many of 'em get well. I've got plenty of witnesses to the fact. Others, it didn't seem to do them a bit of good.

"I've had men come to me that couldn't walk a step. Plenty of people'll tell you that. And in a short while be up walkin', tellin' I cured them. I never done anything. I'm just as blind on that as a man could be. But I'd tell 'em this: there was a power could heal 'em if he would. And I called on him, an' that was Jesus himself.

"You can call it science or anything you please. I'm based on it. My foundation is on Jesus Christ himself.

"I don't belong to no church. But I hope I'm a believin' man. I ain't no infidel. I don't think I will belong to no church.

"Whenever God made the world, he made Adam and gave him dominion over the things in it. That's what the Scripture says—the first of Genesis. Well, dominion means control, don't it? Maybe you can give me light on it. That's the way to control anything, if you start right."

The Faith Healer

"I was down there [by the lake] and heard a car start up hyere by the bear pen about three o'clock in the day. Well, I met a man about halfway. He was a stranger—never saw him before, ain't seen him since. He says, 'Mr. Thrift, I have a man out there I brought to you, a sick man.' I says, 'Where is he?' He says, 'Yonder in the car.'

"Well, we went walkin' right on. I says, 'How'd you know to fetch him to me?' He says, 'People instructed to fetch 'im to you; you'd cure him.' I says, 'Who told you?' He says, 'Mistress Guy.' She'd been to me twice for rheumatic pains. And during this talk we'd been walkin' right straight toward this car, but yet wasn't there.

"We got right about that stump there, Mr. Harper, an' the car was up about the bear pen [forty feet away]. He says to me: 'Mr. Thrift, what kind of religion do you carry?' That's the words he spoke exactly. I says, 'None, as I know of.' He says, 'I never knew any man to do this unless he was a minister of the gospel or some strict sect.'

"I stopped and looked at him in the eye. I turned around to him right then. I said, 'Did you ever know a preacher to do anything like this, sir?' He says, 'I've heard.' I says, 'Well, you can hear anything. But did you ever know, of your own knowledge, a preacher to do anything like this?' He stood there, looked right on the ground betwixt

me an' him, about a minute. He raised his face up an' he looked me right in the eye, an' says, 'I don't know that I ever did, of my own personal knowledge.' And I says, 'No, and I don't expect you ever will.'

"Well, I walked around then to the man claimed to be sick. He didn't get out of the car. An' I spoke to him, told him who I was. I can't go over all the conversation we had. But anyhow, I says to 'im, 'Pardner, by what you've heard of me, if you believe that I could do you any good, beyond a doubt I believe you'll get better. It depends on your own faith. If you ain't got it, it's no use of me to start.' Faith healing, that's what it is—that's what I mean.

"And I told him to write to me about ev'ry two or three weeks. I give him my address. And he wrote to me from time to time, until he said he was well. There was no need of his writing more.

"Now whether I ever done anything, I don't know. I call on the great man, Jesus, that's who I call on. That's who I'm calling on all the time.

"If you'll come to me sick, I'll do all I can. It don't matter whether he's white, black, red, or blue. And it don't cost him nothin'—not a cent. All free. They consult me all around. They touch me on every side. And I could keep on talking or telling you from now until tomorrow morning. And what I tell you, I don't care where you put it. Publish it anywhere you like."

A Bird Clips Uncle Lone's Hair

"I can't tell you the date it was in, but I judge it was about four years ago, along about May. I was seated on the porch there at home, reading a paper. I'd put off my hat and laid it down on a chair where I was setting. I heard something fluttering, flying, about my head. I thought it was a big green muskeeter hawk, catching gnats or insects. But it pitched right on my head, Mr. Harper, and I found it was a bird of some description. It commenced clipping my hair with his mouth, just like he was cutting with scissors. But he was clipping with his teeth—with his mouth . . . like a pair of scissors.

"About a couple of minutes he was back on my head. Cut another mouthful and went again. 'Bout the same length of time he was back again on to my head, clipping. And carried another load.

"About the same length of time he was back again and pitched on the side of a porch post. And he looked just like an English sparrow, only he was gray. More like the color of a dove than anything else.

"He set there, I suppose, half a minute on the post, and there was two dogs laying there on the porch by me. He hopped across the floor and he commenced clipping hair off a dog. Right there at me—not over six feet. He flew around, and the dog scared him, you know. He pitched a few feet off on the floor. He went back to that dog a third time, you know. The dog would scare him again, throw his head around an' scare him off.

"Then he hopped right by that dog and went to the next dog. That dog done the same thing—wheeled his head around and scared him. And he hopped back a second time and tried to clip off it. And the third time he started, he saw the cat a-settin' in the door, a-lookin' at him, about ten feet from him. He looked him close over. He looked him good in the face. The cat was still, you know.

"When he figgered he'd made out that cat, he left. He left right then, too. I saw him setting on a pilin' a few times after that, for the next day or two. And he dis-

appyeared. I think the cat caught him.

"That was as great an experience as I ever had with any wild thing. And I've been in the woods all my life. I never missed a syllable of it. It was just like I told you. The chil'ern was gone. There was nobody there but me. There was not a bit of racket nowhere. He didn't seem to notice me when he was clipping that, anymore than I'd been a dead man. Course I didn't move. . . . Now that's a great thing to think about. It knew I was a living being, all right. It looked me right in the eye. It was gathering something to make a nest of, don't you think?"

An Omen of Death

"One of my brothers had a experience like that once, and it outdone him. He lost one of his chil'ern right after that, an' he was kind of upset about it. His name was John.

"I can't tell you what he was in the swamp for, but I believe he was chipping some boxes [turpentine operation] in the swamp. And he had set down to cool a little—it was in the summertime. You know what a took-bird is? It's a little yellow bird that runs along ahead of you. Runs along and picks up worms. And he hollers 'tick, tick' [possibly a water-thrush].

"One of them flew an' pitched right on his knee. Set there and looked him right in the eyes. He said he turned around an' looked him right in the face. Said he done that several times—repeated that several times.

"Then he flew away, and he never saw any more of him. He told me about this as soon as it happened, soon as he had a chance. He said it worried him—a sign like he was follered, as a warning of some sort.

"And in about two weeks he lost his

oldest child—got sick and died. And after that child died, he seemed plumb satisfied about that bird business.

"It must a been somethin' twenty-five years ago, I expect. Betwixt twenty and twenty-five years ago. It's yeller, with a kind of speckled breast, about the size of a bluebird. Sort of a dirty yeller, not bright."

Uncle Lone had a gift for spinning his yarns with good humor and ease. I recall sitting on Hamp Mizell's porch one evening with about ten other people when he related "That Fuss at an Indian Mound." The porch itself shook with our laughter.

That Fuss at an Indian Mound

"One of the funniest things that ever happened to me concerned an Indian mound. There was a feller used to be working for me in the Okefinokee Swamp, by the name of Berry Barnes. And he had found an Indian mound, you understand. He got after me to let's go an' dig into it. I told him all right, we'd go. So we got an axe and some shovels and went down. We dug down till we got down, I suppose, about three foot deep. And there rise up a pretty heavy thunder cloud—look like it was goin' to rain. So eventcherly, he was diggin' down

Lone Thrift reading to Ardith Thrift on his porch. April 1932.

· 71 ·

in the hole himself, an' the wind rose pretty smart, you know. There was two trees leaning against one another like this [he formed an X] don't you understand? An' while he was diggin', with his head down in the hole, these trees made a fuss together, a very peculiar fuss. It sounded like it was down in the hole. He raised up quick an' looked to me an' says, 'What was that, Mr. Thrift?'

"I says, 'I don't know.' Well, I did, you know, but that's what I told him. He says, 'You know, that fuss was down that hole.' That was the words he said. I says, 'Oh, no, that don't amount to nothing; go ahead an' dig on.' So he dug on a little bit more. Directly it made a fuss again, you know. When it did, he throwed down his shovel and said, 'Mr. Thrift, that thing is sure down in that hole.' He said, 'Let's go.' I says, 'No, man, if there's something in there, I'm going to have it.' I says, 'Give me that shovel.' That feller sit up there and he looked around, and after a while it made another fuss. He says, 'Let's go. I can't stand that racket.' 'Well,' I says, 'I hyearn all my life where there's money buried, there's a fuss to be heard. And I'm goin' to get it out of there.'

"And I dug on till I had just as much fun as I wanted to have. Then I quit. He was too scared to dig an' too scared to leave. He never did know what the fuss was. He talked to me many a time later. I never did let on a-tall. He'd talk serious over that thing. And it was on New Craven Island, right over hyere [to the southeast of Suwannee Lake]."

I have heard no more astounding account of the alligator than the one Uncle Lone shared on June 27, 1929. He told it as we were resting beside Suwannee Lake, where we could always see two or three 'gators lazily floating or swimming about. He began by telling of a strange noise that could be heard for a quarter of a mile. Finally he traced the noise to an alligator. At this point I asked him to wait until I could get my notebook ready for taking down his account, word-for-word.

The Mosquito-Catching Alligator

"Several years I kept hearing that sound from time to time. Why it was just as much like putting your foot on a plank an' letting it slap in the mud, as anything you could think of. When I first heard it, I didn't know what it was. And it passed on for a number of years, I was going to say. Eventually I saw him laying out on the batteries or logs or wherever he's supposed to lay out of a day, *with his mouth open*. An' when his tongue would get covered with musketeers, he'd slap his mouth together like that [slapping his hands together], you see. He'll chew a little bit, it look like. An' then he'd open up again an' keep repeating that. Every time his tongue would get covered, he'd make another bite. That about winds it up, as I know anything about it."

A Snake Fight

"Now I'll tell you about this. I didn't see it, but a feller told me about it. I've forgot his name.

"He said that he saw a small king snake coming along through the field. Apparently he was trailing something. He said he went to a stump where there was a good-sized hole going down in the root, and he went down in there. He said he run afoul of a rattlesnake in there, and the rattlesnake begun to sing. He said the little king snake run out of there in a *terrible* rush. And he left there, he said.

"In a few minutes he come back with the biggest king you ever saw. Said they both went down there in that hole. And he heard the fight take place—rattlesnake singing, and they wrestlin' in there.

"After a bit, he said, everything quieted down. The king snakes come out, both of 'em.

"He went and got him a shovel an' axe, an' dug in. He said they had killed as big a rattlesnake as he ever saw in his life. Killed plumb dead, too. He never moved.

"They kill 'em. They're not a bit afyeard of 'em."

We had just celebrated the birthday of Annie Lou Dill at a feast of fried fish, fried chicken, potato salad, white bread, huckleberry pie, cake, and coffee on June 28, 1929. Uncle Lone and I went over into the creek swamp on the far side of the lake—a dank place whose interesting configurations include swollen stumps and gnarled roots of cypress. The lordly "Kate" (pileated woodpecker) leisurely hammered away high on the trunk of some swamp tree, while the alligator frog chirped and the fish jumped. The roundelay of a Carolina wren, the chirrup of a downy woodpecker, the rattling of cicadas all formed an intimate scene. We climbed a platform some twenty-five feet off the ground—Uncle Lone's "bear stand" which allowed him to keep up with the chase once the dogs were in hot pursuit of the bear.

Clearly bear hunting was one of his favorite subjects. Returning to the dock at the lake, we sat together, and he introduced me to a story that dates to Civil War times, one he had heard first at the knee of his father, Robert Thrift. The story he told that day and the other yarn that follows are only two of the many bear stories he would tell over the years.

A Bear Chase on Cowhouse Island

"Have you ever been to the Cowhouse? Well, do you know where Britt Crews lives? This happened right where he lives, in the Cowhouse.

"My father said the bears had killed all of his hogs but five sows. And they had come home and was laying under some rail stacks by the house, about fifty yards away.

"One morning he decided he'd kill a beef for meat. It took him all day to butcher the beef, cut up, and salt down. With the coming of dusk, he goes to feed the horse. Mother was in the kitchen, trying to fix up a little supper. And the dwelling house was betwixt the kitchen and the lot. So when he got down among the corn shucks, a rattling them, mother hollered from the kitchen: the bear had a hog. He made no answer. He didn't think anything to it, you know. She called him a second time and told him a bear had a hog. But he hollered back to her that the hogs was fighting over the jawbones of the beef that he had throwed over the fence.

"But the third time she called him, she got out of the house where she could see him. And she hollered: 'I tell you to come hyere, the bear's got a hog!' Well, then he said he just poked his head out of the door an' looked where the hog was squealing. He said he saw the bear gwine for the swamp. It was a big sow, an' he was toting it, too.

"Well, he run then for his gun. One barrel loaded. He'd shot the beef with one barrel. But he said he took after him. When the bear would run, he'd run. The bear stopped, he'd stop. And he said that bear had the sow through the back, had ketched her about midway so she was balanced.

"He'd gallop with her just like a pony horse. Go about fifty yards, and then he'd lay down an' rest. During this resting time he could gain a little on him. Well, he run him that way, I figger it must-a-been a quarter of a mile or six-hundred yards. And he said he laid the sow down now and run through a little flat—about ten steps from the main scrub. That time when he stopped, father stopped right behind a tree. And the bear, he left the hog and walked right off in the swamp. He said he could have shot him with a long shot, but he didn't know why he didn't do it. He couldn't give his reason. But he could still hear him running about yonder in the scrub.

"In a few minutes he walked right back by the hog—didn't stop—come right straight to him, straight as anything could come, within about ten steps of him. And he rared up, just about as high as he could. An' the way father described it, when he got about as tight [stretched] as he thought he was going to get, he let him have it. Then the bear run just like a horse, it looked like, right back into the scrub. And he must have run against something, and then everything hushed in there.

"Then father said he went, when everything got quiet, to the sow. He got down on the sow, to see whether she'd die, or whether he could raise her. He said he met his thumb and middle finger under the backbone in five places. Bear'd squshed the ribs right in. About this time he heard the bear coming, he thought. He said he rise and run just as fast as he could. Right then he left there. And he looked back an' he seed the bear coming. When he did, he said he got faster. Directly he looked back and the black bear was still closeter it seem,

and he got faster. Eventcherly he said it overtook him. And when it did, it *passed* him.

"And it was a black dog. He'd heard the gun and got into the scrub. But father thought it was a bear all the time.

"Well, he then walked seven miles, Mr. Harper, and back to get a slow trailing dog to trail him up. He went that night and back home before morning—he, the dog with his master.

"And they found him not over twenty steps in the scrub from the hog. He was right there. Looked like he run his head right into a stump and turned a somerset.

"Did you ever know anything about an ol' fashioned corded bedstead? Well, they're made just like those others, but the big wood's on the side. They bore a hole through here, and one here, and one there. And they check a rope through it, like making up a gill net, with about an eight-inch mash. That bear hide, after its legs was cut off and the hide squared up, made a hide for that corded bedstead. Just covered up, just made a fit for a double bed. Just like a cowhide. I've seen it.

"And the bear story was told by father— R. T. Thrift—and I'm satisfied the story was just like he told it. He was supposed to be one of the most responsible men in the county. He always told a straight yarn, and done the straight thing. You ask ernother man, and he'll tell you the same thing.

"My father some kind of killed 'em bears; there's no foolishness about it. He was a still-hunting man; didn't run 'em with dogs. He said his father killed more before him. But I'm satisfied he killed more bear around the swamp here than any other man in the county.

"Ol' man Obadiah Barber was a terrible man. He could of told you some powerful yarns. Uncle Barber [a renowned bear hunter] was inclined to stretch a little, make it a little worse than it was."

A Bear, Tiger-cat, and Buzzards on Floyds Island

"I think it was in the fall of eighteen and ninety-two. 'Long in the first of the cool weather—I think it was in November. Now Floyds Island is about the heart of the swamp. I was on a trip fur-huntin', by myself.

"In the meanwhile I decided in my mind I'd go to the island an' stay a night, don't you see? I had two dogs with me. There's a little landing on the cane bed, where you run the boat up in. And the old dog, he got right out an' went to the old camp where he was used to going. I think it was a gum tree, stood in the cane only six or eight feet from where my boat was. And when the other dog got out on the right-hand side, he found something right there.

"I could hear the thing moving in there—a big thing, but I couldn't tell what it was. And eventcherly it made a motion, didn't run right at the dog. And the dog jumped right out in the boat, on my feet. Then the old dog come. They put in bayin' right there. An' eventcherly I found it was moving a little, gwine down the cane-brake. Well, I jumped out an' run round the hammock to cut it off. When I started, it give a scare; I reckon it did. It beat me to the stand by the old camping ground, about a hundred and fifty yards from there. He passed it before I could make it.

"Well, after a while, the old dog come back. And the dog found somethin' I thought was a swamp rabbit in a little bay scrub clump. And he'd run around, keep peekin' in like he saw a rabbit. So I was standing with my hand on the gun.

"And the other dog come then, so all three of us was there. The dog went on the other side of the clump and dive in there. Well, when he did, it run right by me as close as your feet there [two yards]. It was a tiger-cat. Did you ever see one? No? They're red—near about bright red, about as big as a cur dog, with a white stripe hyere at his eyes. Well, he dodged them dogs right now. He got away. Well, that kinder got me scared—me a young feller in there by myself. That kinder scared me out.

"Well, I looked up in the gum trees there, an' I expect there was fifty head of buzzards settin' there. I couldn't think of nothing but a panther had killed a deer there. That's all I could think of. But it give me such excitement, I didn't investigate. I left there. But I moved right out in the prairie in a little bulk—a little clump—and camped there all night. Water all around me.

"The second day I got out. I went home then. And I told the story, you understand. My father said he'd go back with me. We went right on back down there. Carried just one dog with us.

"Well, when we got in there . . . I heard that thing get up, and it walked just like a man. I couldn't have told it from a man, by the walk. Walked a few feet and ketched a tree. . . . Father he looks around at me, you know, an' says: 'You know, I believe that's some ol' runaway feller layin' out in hyere.' That kind of give some kind of excitement for a few minutes.

"But I told him I didn't hardly think so, that it must be a bear, to be sure. We went on up where it left, put the dog behind it. He run it off in that heavy cane-brake, where he commenced to bayin' in again. He didn't bay long before he come back. I called him out. I told father we'd stay all night an' go up yonder next morning.

· 75 ·

"We didn't find anything more [the next day]. I told father we was fixing to leave. We got nearby that place. Father hold the dog till I got around where we cut him off before. . . .

"Dog commenced baying right by that tree. He stayed right in one place. Wouldn't swim. He'd look in the water there and bay.

"Well, I didn't see nothing much. I told father, 'Let's go.' I thought the bear or whatever it was had left. We went on down and got in the boat and started. I called the dog. Dog wouldn't come. He kept baying. The more I'd call, the worse he'd get. We was about two-hundred yards away from where the dog was.

"I told father I was going back. That he was a baying something, if it was nothin' but an alligator. He'd found somethin'. Well, I walked right on straight to him as I could. It was about two-hundred yards. I got up, I suppose, in a hundred feet of the dog. I was looking right at the dog, too.

"Dog was baying something on the other side of him from me. I got my gun in shoot-ing position. Look like the dog walked right straight toward it. I think I was at least in ten short steps of him.

"A bear riz right up out of the water an' run off. The dog right behind him. I couldn't shoot for the dog. He was right in the way.

"The dog kept follering an' baying him. Father come. We never got close enough to shoot him. We couldn't see him in that cane, you understand, till we both give out an' quit.

"But those buzzards got up in the trees, like I been telling you about.

"We come back and investigated there, to see what was the trouble. We found an alligator skin, rolled up an' ready for ship-ping. And we found where the bear had been lyin' right in the water, minding the buzzards off'n that 'gator skin.

"[Later] I saw the man that said he lost a 'gator hide there. Hardy Sweat was the man. Well, it had been three weeks from the time Sweat had been there till the time father an' me went back."

OWEN THRIFT · 1852–1931

When I came to know him in 1929, he was probably the most delightfully simple, old-fashioned resident of the Okefinokee area within the circle of my acquaintances. His nature was a compound of friendliness, humor, and homely philosophy. Like his nephew Lone Thrift, he was a man of marked individuality, true to his own way of life, and independent in his thinking. He was one to whom those immortal lines of Horace might apply with particular aptness:

Beatus ille qui procul negotiis,
ut prisca gens mortalium,
paterna rura bobus exercet suis,
solutus omni faenore.

Happy he who far removed from the affairs of
    commerce,
like the ancient race of mortal man,
toils in the ancestral fields with his own oxen,
released from all the claims of money.

The only exception would be that, in Uncle Owen's case, the oxen were replaced by a faithful old horse, of an age at least comparable to his own (the late seventies), and—like Uncle Owen—distinctly individualistic in character. It was a pure delight to record my old friend's homely, genial words—especially such a one as "muzog"—which I heard from him for the first time. His archaic speech had never been contaminated by attending a motion-picture show.

Hamp Mizell took me to Uncle Owen's place on June 29, 1929. We rode in his Ford and talked of this old timer we were going to visit. Arriving at his place near the swamp in the vicinity of Suwannee Lake, I noticed his log-built home had a mud-and-stick chimney—a rarity even in 1929. A rail fence enclosed the house and garden. Here were some fig trees whose luscious fruit Hamp and I enjoyed.

Uncle Owen, at age seventy-seven, had been to see a doctor a few times but had never called one to his home except on one occasion: after suffering a black widow spider's bite. He was as healthy as his beloved old gray horse, of whom he spoke affectionately.

"We've laid away. My old horse made the crop all right. That's the best horse in the

Owen Thrift and "the best horse in the world" preparing to travel homeward from Suwannee Lake. June 1929.

world. Till I moved up on the creek, I never planted a pertater with a plough in my life. I ain't felt good this week like I generally do. The ol' horse ploughed me a little too hard. Got me too hot. The flies bothers him. But take him out where he expects to plough all day, he'll be slow. But if the flies flinders him, he'll work faster. If you talk to him, he'll pay all the attention you want him to. If he's heavy-loaded, he won't let you tote a whip."

On and on we talked while some of the womenfolk were preparing dinner; some of them, however, could not resist hearing Uncle Owen and joined us on the porch. Like most older swampers, he had a large stock of bear stories and tales of the days on the Georgia frontier.

The Gun Wouldn't Fire

"My ol' father, he come hyere right after the Indians was gone. It's sixty years ago, or sixty-five years, I expect.

"There come a bear in the night close up to the plantation and ketched a hog. And my old father got up an' went out there an' shot him where he had the hog. And the bear run off. There come three dogs running from the house, and they went afoul of the bear an' put him up a tree. Daddy, he went there with his old flint-and-steel rifle, and went a-snapping at the bear.

"The gun wouldn't fire. And the bear come down to the dogs and the old man. So he went up there and put in with his gun—beating him with his gun. And the bear put back up the tree. And he just kept a-coming down, and the dogs a-gnawing him. And Daddy a-fighting him with his gun. Finally he went back up the tree and stayed.

"But by this time the old man had no part of his gun but the barrel. He'd beat all the rest off, and it was gone. Knocked all the lock, stock, an' everything else off but the barrel. And he hollered an' squalled, and the dogs barked till it waked an old man up at the house. And he took a gun and come down there and killed it.

"That winds it up, but the old man's name was Carr W. Thrift. He was my father. Bob Partin hunted with him, and he was an Injun-mixed man—had Injun blood. As for my old father, he was one of the frontierers here, right down on the swamp, somewhere around eight-five or ninety years ago, right at the edge of a hunderd. Born an' raised in Washington County within thirty mile of Macon."

The Best Man in Waresboro

"This feller John Snider was raised in Washington County. And finally after the people moved in hyere and settled, why he come out hyere to this country. An old feller hired him to work for him.

"People was powerful to fight here in them days. And this old man went to this little town Waresboro [west of Waycross, Georgia], and he was a-telling these fighting men what a man he had at his place. And they says to him, 'Well, you oughter fetched him out. And we'd a-whipped him for you today.' He says, 'Well, he'll be hyere this evening. . . . Boys, you better let him alone when he comes.'

"So after a little while Snider walked up, and pretty soon they raised a row with him. And he knocked one down an' run at another an' bit him on the chin, till his lip dropped down hyere, till it hung down. And he jumped off to one side and picked up a whiskey barrel by the chines—what little bit of the stave that sticks up above the groove. It was an empty barrel, you know, and he picked it up in his teeth, and throwed it over his head. And he says to them, 'Boys, I'm the best man ever footed Waresboro.' My old daddy did say that he was the best man, for his manhood, he ever seed in his life.

"Now I've seen my old man come in just as bloody from fighting as if he'd butchered a beef. And he'd be in a good humor, too. He didn't hold no grudge. And he said it was all right if the other man could whip him. No man could do nothing with him, unless he was just able to overpower him. He was a man who'd fight with sticks or with his hands. Wouldn't drink a-tall."

Unable to resist these accounts of frontier life, I asked Uncle Owen to tell us more. He took up where he had left off without hesitation.

"It was seldom in my raising hyere that you would see a man drunk. They were mighty scattering. They would go to log-rollings and workings, and the man of the house would have some liquor. You'd never see a man tote a bottle of liquor. As for a young man, he thought it was a teetotal disgrace for people to know he had ever been drunk in his life. They just thought it was a final disgrace to get drunk. The womenfolks wouldn't have nothing to do with him. . . . That was just the way with me, 'cause I was raised hyere.

"In my raising, there was no school house to get no education. I went to school maybe about three months. No, I just got enough education for it to bother me.

"I was born about twenty-five mile from here, on an island [Cowhouse] in the Okefinokee. Stayed till . . . just as I was getting

grown. Stayed on the first place I carried the old lady to, twenty-five year. . . . And I hyere to tell you I know about as much as anybody about it. The land produces pretty good stuff when we have seasonable weather. Hogs used to do mighty well hyere in the woods. About as many again cattle now in the woods as there ought to be."

The house and yard were full of Uncle Owen's curious contrivances. There was a "steel mill" for grinding corn, "battlin' sticks," and the old wash tub. The latches on the gates were made of iron, and some sort of spring kept them in place—the handiwork of Uncle Owen, who said that he could "tinker like everything." He maintained not one but two well-sweeps. His grounds contained luscious mulberries, figs, and peaches. The yard's beauty was enhanced by "Lagerstreamer" (crepe myrtle). Across the way was the scuppernong arbor, and in the arbor somebody had hung a bear paw.

After spending part of the morning of May 20, 1930 at the Thrift place, Mrs. Thrift accompanied us on our return trip to Suwannee Lake, where she would stay for several days. Meanwhile Uncle Owen had gone to Lone Thrift's to have a tooth pulled. When he met us later at Hamp's house, he said this was the very first time he and his wife had left their children at the same time. And they had been married for more than a half century!

At the dinner table that evening, Uncle Owen commented on a variety of subjects: "People say, 'How you getting along, Mr. Thrift?' I says, 'I'm getting 'long very well.' I never find no difference. I about got the same thing all the time. So I ain't seen much difference. Now in war times, at Hopkins, I could step over there an' get me all I wanted. As far as money, I kept all of mine I could. And most of 'em [fellow tur-penters] blowed theirs in. I never have seen no need of using anything before you needed it. Them high prices in the war holp me a lot."

During the evening, while we were sit-ting once more on Hamp's porch, Mrs. Thrift (age seventy-five) was persuaded to tell the following story about an adventure two boys had with an alligator. It happened long ago at the ford of Black River, just out-side the swamp on the northwestern side.

The 'Gator Had the Boy by the Head

"Henry Bennett went down there to go in swimming—him and his brother. They climb up on this stump to jump off in there. And one of 'em jumped off ahead of the other. And he waited for him to rise before he jumped in. He wouldn't jump in because his brother wouldn't rise. And directly he seed his brother's foot come up. He jumped in then an' gathered his brother by the foot. He knew there was something the matter with him. And he drug him, 'gator an' all, out to dry land. The 'gator had the boy by the head, but turned him loose when they got out to the land. Then they went to the house and got a gun an' shot him. And I see the boy many a time with the scars on both sides of his head that long [three inches]. An' there weren't no hair on the scars. They showed all right, back on his head."

The Thrifts provided little new factual information on the history of the swamp and the people, but their stories and say-ings, of course, are themselves a kind of

history. Two bits of information, however, came forth on this day. Mrs. Thrift con-firmed an account heard all around the swamp that alligators once were so numer-ous on Billys Lake that one could have walked across on "'gator heads." Uncle Owen recounted the tradition that, before the Civil War (he said "Confederate War"), there were few settlers in the area of the Okefinokee: "Just once in a while a man settled about. An' by the time it was wound up, there was hardly any men left— just a passel of women and chil'ern."

On July 13, 1931 we had the pleasure of Uncle Owen's company for a mere hour or so. Late in the afternoon when we walked up the pleasant road from the lake through the piney woods to Lone Thrift's place, we unexpectedly found Uncle Owen. He was waiting for Uncle Lone to pull yet another tooth. He said that his friend and relative Lone was the only man in "these parts" who had "pullikins" [forceps].

Uncle Owen was as picturesque as ever in speech and in appearance. Dressed in regulation blue shirt and overalls, he cov-ered his head with a gray felt hat. On his feet he wore a much-patched pair of leather slippers. No socks, I believe. Out of habit he carried an old sawed-off shotgun with a single barrel and a firing mechanism of hammer and percussion cap. He had cut down a double-barrel model and tied the weapon together with wire over wooden patches. He carried the gun over his shoul-der on a sling of white cord. He could reach the gun quickly, and he did so when shoot-ing snakes. Over the other shoulder he slung a wallet for shot and powder. This in the year 1931.

Preparing to leave, I noticed he was chewing tobacco right on. He said he'd never had a tooth filled in his life. Then he asked me the time and when the sun would set. Since my watch said 6 P.M., I speculated that the sun would be setting about eight o'clock. Knowing he could travel all the way home in the light, he began his journey. What a picture he made!

EZEKIEL S. HENDERSON · 1857–1952(?)

Here was a prize contributor to Okefinokee lore. He talked of 'gators and bears, quoted fragments of ballads, and reminisced about original settlers of the swamp. I met him on May 23, 1930, when he and his wife had come to Suwannee Lake for a day's fishing. He seemed to enjoy talking about the old days and was jubilant about seeing his words recorded on paper. Uncle Zeke started by laughing about Si Mixon, an

Mr. and Mrs. Ezekiel (Zeke) S. Henderson with Lone Thrift at Suwannee Lake. May 1930.

original character who lived at Mixon Ferry, where the Suwannee flows out of the Okefinokee.

"One time there was a surveying party down on the Suwannee River, a party of gover'ment men. They had wagon trains in them days. And one of the mules got sick. Old Si Mixon told 'em what kind of prescription would cure them of the colic. Told 'em to take Gibson salts and *blue pervittle*—vittle [vitriol] is what he meant—and mix it up all together, I think, with a pint of water. Get the desired ingredients, and it'd be sure to have the desired effect. But there was a lawyer along, an' he said the funny part about Si Mixon's prescription was the ingredient *pervittle*. You could hear that lawyer laugh a half a mile.

"Now Si Mixon's sister, Patsy Covington, she went to the camp and told 'em that they should pull up and go close to brother Si, as he was the only man there that could talk quality. But they didn't go. They stayed at our place, and they didn't go to hear Si talk quality.

"We lived down there near Mixon Ferry a couple of years. That was in '78 and '79. Major Mahan was in charge of the party. They finally moved into Billys Island and set up their headquarters there. Jim Lee [Zeke's uncle by marriage] lived there then. Jim Henderson [Zeke's brother] stayed in there several years; helped him farm. But I was raised out here about six mile of Waycross. I live in town now."

Dan'l Spikes was another early swamper known by Uncle Zeke. This fellow Spikes was the one who inspired William Tennyson Chesser's locally famous swamp ballad by the same name. Uncle Zeke said that Dan'l arrived on Chessers Island before the Chessers moved there in the 1850s. He be-

came a draft resister during the Civil War. In his later years he lived in Millwood, some seventeen miles west of Waycross. One day, when he was eleven years old, he said to his old mother: "'Mammy, found me an ol' bar [barrow, a castrated hog] today. God damn me if he ain't as big as a cow.'" It had been lost for six or seven years, and in the meantime it had presumably been leading a feral life.

While Uncle Zeke was unable to recall any of the words of Chesser's "Dan'l Spikes," he said he had "been studying at a ballad, and I think it come from England, too":

When first to this country a stranger I came,
Nobody knew me nor knew not my name.
I fell in love with a pretty maiden.
And she said to uncart your horses
And feed 'em some hay.

Chorus:
Pretty Polly, pretty Polly, would you think it
  unkind,
To set down by the side of you and tell you my
  mind?

And she replied: 'My mind is to marry and
  never part,
For the first time I saw you, you wounded my
  heart.
Unharness your horses and give 'em some hay,
And you can set aside of me what time you do
  stay.'

(repeat chorus)

"Don't remember the title. Don't know of a soul that would know it, since the old folks are all dead. My mother knew that. That was a love song in her days. She lived to eighty-five. I learned the song from her. It would do to call it a ballad." He said the song went on to describe "what comfort he could show her in married life. It was a real pretty song."

As we talked, he went on to relate stories about the Okefinokee and its wildlife. Two of the tales that follow recall the numerous alligators that once were said to inhabit Billys Lake near the Lees' home.

Thick with 'Gators

"I was fishing one time in Billys with my old uncle [Jim Lee]. I was doing the rowing and he was doing the fishing. The 'gators made such a racket I didn't know what it was. And he told me it was the 'gators a-muddying Big Bonnet Lake by Billys Lake. He told me to paddle easy and not hit the boat with the paddle, so we'd slip up on 'em and not disturb 'em and see 'em fishing. We got around a little clump of bushes in plain of Big Bonnet Lake, and they must have been somewhere between one and two thousand of the 'gators. Bonnet Lake was about four or five acres big. And them 'gators would rise and jump their length and go down. The bottom of Bonnet Lake is a soft mud. And it was easy to muddy. And they all muddy at the same time, and then stop at the same time and go to fishing [for] just a few breaths. They was jumping and sloshing. They'd go down to the bottom and dig up the mud and scatter it with their tails. And then they'd go to fishing again.

"I remember one tremendous big alligator that rose up in the water with a trout in his mouth, about twelve or fourteen pounds. Had him crossways in his mouth. And he just moved up to the bank and jammed against the bank until he got him head first in his mouth, and then swallowed him.

"That was the first time I was ever there when there was so many 'gators. And I've seen the 'gators so thick, it looked like if you'd been out of the boat and if the 'gators had held your weight, you could walk all over the lake on 'gator heads. . . . Of course I didn't count the 'gators but I'm satisfied, time we got to the end of the lake, there'd been five thousand."

A Bear Swims a Gauntlet of 'Gators

"Me and the same man, Uncle Jim Lee, was fishing again. In about the widest part of the lake [two hundred feet], a tremendous big bear walked in and swum the lake about a couple er hunderd yards from us. And we drove the 'gators again. Their heads was thick all over the water. And the big 'gators, looked like, would start to catch him. They was fourteen or fifteen feet long. I didn't see no small ones start after him at all. He'd rare right up in the water, take both forefeet out and slam right down on the 'gator's head and swim right on. And I made the remark to my uncle, that 'It'll be one less bear in the Okefinokee Swamp right now. He is going to get caught.' But he went through safe and walked out on the land on the other side. They'd come fronting him, and he'd just push 'em right down. He was a great big bear, a great big feller."

A Tremendous Bear, A Tremendous Dog

"Reckon I better give you the name of the hunting party to start with. The party was J. W. Mixon, Dump Griffin, Jim Henderson, and myself. And we come to where a bear had killed a hog. We was starting to hunting on Rowell Island. And we had the best bear dog and deer dog combined I ever saw. And his name was 'Dog.' He was half bull and half cur—a big old red-eyed dog. Weighed about a hunderd and twenty-five pound. Biggest dog I ever saw in my life.

"The bear had eat a square mess of the hog and was laying nearby where he'd killed the hog. And the dog run onto him. And it was right close to the edge of the swamp. He run into the swamp about a hunderd yards and went up a cypress.

"At the root of the cypress grew up these bamboo vines [*Smilax*] profusely—made a big bulk around it. Just as we got in sight of the cypress, we saw the bear going through the bamboo briar, up the cypress. We discovered he was carrying a dog with him. The dog had him by the ham, and he carried the dog up the tree about forty foot high. We couldn't shoot the bear for hitting the dog. Everybody was looking and hating for the dog to get killed. He was the best dog we had on the hunt.

"He'd hold the bear's ham, and he'd swing off from the tree, trying to jerk the bear off. And after a while his jaws give out, and he had to turn the bear loose.

"And he struck in the bamboo-briar bed and scrambled through it to get to the ground, and he never got hurt one bit. But we proceeded to kill the bear. Everybody wouldn't believe a bear story like that unless they'd been through it just like I have.

"Such a tremendous big bear, and such a tremendous dog!

"It was about eighteen hunderd an' eighty-eight. I don't care if you publish it. It's so. I'm the only eye-witness living to the bear carrying the dog up the tree. The worst looking dog you ever saw in your life. Look like he could whip a lion. Aw, he was severe!"

RHODA MIZELL SPAULDING · 1876–1948

"Aunt Rhodie" was how we all knew her. This elder sister of Hamp Mizell was born in May 1876 on the eastern border of the swamp a few miles north of Camp Cornelia. Her paternal grandfather had lived in Brantley County and had died at his home on the bend of the St. Marys River. He was a veteran of the "Indian War." One of her ancestors was said to have come from France and to have married an Indian. She doesn't know where he lived. Her Uncle Isaac, too young to enlist, ran away to the Civil War and was never heard from again. Her father already had gone to the war.

While many of her relatives fought in the Civil War, she knew about some deserters who hid out in the interior of the swamp. Tradition was that a certain John ———— fled from authorities by hiding along the Big Bend of the St. Marys River: "They said he had a worse time than if he had gone in the army."

Her father, Josiah Mizell, brought back some songs from Civil War battlefields. One was "The Girl I Left behind Me." But most of her father's songs seemed to have been of local origins, such as the one he sang each morning as he made the rounds waking up his sons:

Wake up, Jacob,
Wake up, John.

Let's go huntin'
Ter kill them coons
What's eatin' our punkins.

We were sitting on her back porch one evening when she recited a version of *Barb'rie Allen.* She had learned it from David Yarborough, a son of Ben, along about 1901. It was only within a few days that I learned from others that people had been singing this song "forever" in the swamp.

Her family was steeped in the history, folklore, music, and traditions of the Okefinokee. Her father, two uncles, three brothers, and a cousin were experienced fiddlers. In this pleasant environment she became acquainted quite early with the domestic affairs of an Okefinokee household, the crops of the surrounding fields, the fruit and 'yarbs' of the home garden, the neighborly customs and the religious practices of the sparse community, the conspicuous elements of the local animal and plant life, and the old songs and ballads that were prominent features of the Okefinokee heritage.

Like many women of the Okefinokee, Aunt Rhodie transmitted a body of lore about various cures and medicines, but she

Aunt Rhodie, with her granddaughter, feeding a litter of pigs at Suwannee Lake. No date.

did not seem to "take much stock" in most of them. She recited these "cures" as examples of old folk medicine in the swamp. They're not recommended for anyone in this age of advanced medical knowledge. In fact, some of the plants mentioned by Aunt Rhodie can be deadly.

Bad Colds

"Take leaves of Catnip and boil 'em and make a tea. Used for colds. Causes them to perspire."

Kidney Trouble

"Use Pennyr'yal [Pennyroyal?] tea for kidney trouble. Then there was that stuff mama used to have in the garden—called it Yarrer [Yarrow?]."

Measles

"Sassafras tea will make measles break out on you."

A Purgative

"Boneset tea's used as a purgative for bilious folks. Grows down by the field, along the fences" [same plant as "agueweed" and "feverwort"].

Blood Purifier

"Queen's delight" [*Stillingia sylvatica*].

Sick Stomach

"Use Snakeroot for a sick stomach."

Sore Throat

"Red-oak bark is good. Make a gargle for sore throat."

Fevers

"Sage tea, used warm for fever. Used cold for night sweats. Some people used that for meat—for flavoring sausage."

Baby's Thrash

"When the baby takes the thrash [fever accompanied by reddening of the throat] . . . there's a yellow thrash and a white thrash. You go out in the morning before sun-up, while the baby's still a-sleeping. Go east of the house and you get a pine top with dew on it. And you take that in. And you shake the dew off this pine top in the baby's face. Then you take this pine top and put it in the chimney. And you let it stay there till it dies (you know, till the straw dies). Then the thrash'll be well on the child. Call it Hindu witchcraft.

"Another remedy for thrash is to take persimmon root and low-bush myrtle roots and shumate [*Sumac*] bark. Boil that and make a tea, and sweeten it with honey. Make a little mop of cloth, and wet the mop with that tea, and mop their mouths out with that. That was for the thrash, too.

"Take nine doodle-bugs and string 'em alive around the neck. And wear 'em for nine days. They use that for the thrash, too."

Aunt Rhodie was kindness itself, not only in imparting to me her own knowledge of old times in the swamp and in singing various songs and ballads, but as a genuine personal friend. I first became acquainted with her in 1921 on Billys Island, where she was assisting in the operation of a food-dispensing establishment for the lumber company's employees. After 1930 she lived at Suwannee Lake in a cottage next to her brother Hamp. She was a devoted "other mother" to his children, and they were strongly attached to her.

The last time I saw Aunt Rhodie was in August 1944. When I approached her with the idea of recording one of her favorite songs for the collection of folk music in the Library of Congress, she consented graciously. She chose a thoroughly charming and wit-filled piece that she had learned from a girlhood friend, Miss Mamie Shivers. The song was "My Grandmother Lived on Yonder Little Hill." It was an admirable performance for a woman of sixty-eight years.

My Grandmother Lives on Yonder Little Hill

1. My grand- mother lives on yon-der lit-tle hill, As

fine an old la-dy as ev-er I seen, she has

of- ten cau- -tioned me with care, An'

all false young men to be- ware,

Refrain:

ti-mi-ay, ti-mi-o, ti-mi, ti-mi, ti-mi, um-a-tum

All false young men to be- ware.

2. These false young men they'll flatter and they coax,
   Tell you they love you, you better be aware,
   They' flatter and they'll coax 'til they ketch you in a snare,
   An' that's the way it goes fo' grandma's care.

   Ti-mi-ay, ti-mi-o, ti-mi, ti-mi, ti-mi, um-a-tum,
   That's the way it goes fo' grandma's care.

3. O, the first come a-courtin' was little Johnny Green,
   Fine a little feller as ever I seen,
   But my grandmother's words kept a-ringin' in my head,
   Couldn't understand one word that he said.

   Ti-mi-ay, ti-mi-o, ti-mi, ti-mi, ti-mi, um-a-tum,
   Couldn't understand one word that he said.

4. O, the next come a-courtin' was young Andy Grove
   And there I met with my heart's first love,
   With my joyous love I couldn't be afraid,
   Better to get married than to die an old maid.

   Ti-mi-ay, ti-mi-o, ti-mi, ti-mi, ti-mi, um-a-tum,
   Better to get married than to die an old maid.

5. I've often thought there was some mistake
   What a noise these old folks make
   If the boys and the girls had of all a-been afraid
   Grandma herself would have been an old maid.

   Ti-mi-ay, ti-mi-o, ti-mi, ti-mi, ti-mi, um-a-tum,
   Grandma herself would have been an old maid.

ROBERT ALLEN CHESSER · 1859–1929

He was a mighty hunter, a peerless raconteur, a homely philosopher, a locally renowned maker of cane syrup, a fiddler, a banjo-picker, a faithful Hardshell, and more. He embodied the abundant life of the Okefinokee. It was my privilege to know Uncle Allen in his home surroundings during two brief summers of his later years. Five decades later his sayings remain a matter of frequent quotation in our family. I think particularly of his simple and earnest saying of grace: "Thank the Lord for what we have to eat." He would follow quickly with this: "Now, boys, turn up your plates. There's the hominy; hyere's the gravy!"

In days before the Civil War, Allen Chesser's forebears lived in Liberty (now Long) County, Georgia. That county in-cluded among its inhabitants the LeContes, McIntoshes, Stewarts, Joneses, and other distinguished families. But the 1850 census includes no mention of the Chessers as slave owners. Like the vast majority of Georgia's backwoodsmen at the time, they were yeoman farmers, woodsmen, and hunters. It was Allen's father, William Tennyson Chesser, who migrated to the swamp in search of "good range, good water, and good health," as he often said. Allen's older brother, Samuel Archie (1854–1924), claimed the northern end of Chessers Island and Allen claimed the lower end upon the death of their father in 1896.

Early each morning Uncle Allen was in the habit of footing it slowly along the path through the hammock, with his favorite walking-stick of "hoorah-bush" in hand,

"A mighty hunter, a peerless raconteur, a homely philosopher, a locally renowned maker of cane syrup, a fiddler, a banjo-picker, a faithful Hardshell, and more." Robert Allen Chesser poses on the porch of his boyhood home on Chessers Island in 1922.

and dropping in for a little visit at our camp. His hunting days were over; no longer was his strength equal to poling a boat along the Okefinokee waterways. His usual response to an inquiry about his well-being was, "I'm feeling mighty tough this morning."

As his hunting activities came to a gradual close, perhaps his finest art—that of raconteur—throve the more. Less diffident than some of the older swampers, he was not only willing but apparently pleased at the idea of these verbatim transcriptions of his stories. "If all that I've seen in the Okefinokee was put in a book," he mused, "it'd be right interesting. And the pretty part of it, every bit of it's the truth." He had a natural slowness of speech, and he willingly paused between sentences for me to catch up with him. There came a morning when he spoke meaningfully: "Some day, when I'm feeling better than I am now, I want to tell you the story of that biggest bear fight I ever got into." That was in the summer of 1921.

I was back on Chessers Island again for a summer's work in 1922. During this long second summer in his company, my acquaintance with Uncle Allen grew into a rather intimate friendship. That summer the day for the bear story came at last. Uncle Allen came to see us and sat on the ground in a shady spot beneath a live oak. "Now I'll tell you about that bear fight if you'll get your book," he said as he settled in to tell this epic from his Okefinokee boyhood.

That Was My Initiation

"I must tell you how we come to go. I was a boy, I reckon ten or twelve years old, and the other boys was older. I was off with my bow and arrow somewheres, and they went off and left me; took the gun and the dogs.

"They left one gun, and it was an old flint-and-steel. As true a shooting gun as I ever shot, too. I'd taken that gun, and went to Hurst Island. Well, when I walked out on that island, I didn't have to look. There was a bear *right there*. And I, you know, could have killed it with all ease if I had a mind to, if I had the sense I have now, but I thought I had to be right close on to him.

"And while I was a slipping to get closer to him, he jumped up a tree. He went about two jumps up the tree (I could hear his paws hit the tree), and slung his head off on each side, *thisaway* an' *thataway*, and then he come down. He took his time, and went noselin about, feeding on the pameeter [saw-palmetto] buds. And he drifted off in the bay, and me along after him, trying to get a chance to shoot. Poking along and feeding along. As far as he went, I went. And I got, I reckon, in about ten steps of him. Lost all my good chances to kill him out on the island, and had him there in that bay. I couldn't see nothing of him but his head. When I decided to shoot, I aimed through the bushes to strike his body, and I shot. Of course, them kind of ball is easy turned. And of course I missed him clear—never touched him.

"So I stood still, and so did the bear. And he stood there, I reckon, something like a few breaths. And he commenced grumbling, growling. I could hear him just as plain in his manner. And the notion struck me, I had better get out of that bay. So I went, and I went in a hurry, too. I didn't look for a bear or nothing, only for a way to get out of that bay *quick*. I got out to the island. The island was burnt off, and the grass was only about that high [one foot], looked pretty and green. So I went out about, I reckon, seventy-five yards on the island.

"The notion struck me I better load my gun. And I sat my gun down just like that [slanted, with butt touching ground], and I was a-pouring my charge of powder in. And I raised my head and looked back to see if I could see anything of the bear; and sure enough, he come right on my trail.

"So I pulled out my knife and opened it, and stuck it in the ground beside me, so if I come in close contact, I'd have a chance to use it. I kept loading then just as fast as I could—I kept the balls loose in my pocket—and a-looking for the bear. And he kept a-coming too.

"There was an old log that had fell, lying just like that, and he come to the top of the log, and he was a-gnawing on them limbs, popping the limbs and throwing the bark off'n them."

I asked Uncle Allen, "What did he do that for?"

"He was mad. He walked just like a billy goat. You've seen them when they're mad—feel biggity [tense with anger]? And he had his ears hugged right close to his head, just *thataway*, and I was setting about four or five steps from the stump of that tree. And he got through gnawing there at the other end of the log. He raised his head up, just looked right at me, just as straight as he could do it. And he grinned. And I could see his teeth a-shining just as pretty and white. Didn't open his mouth, just there with his ears laid back.

"He started to walk then, right aside of the log, till he got to the stump. And then he put in to gnaw on it, just like he had on the top. He'd be a-gnawing on me in a minute, I thought, and me a-loading all that time. I was about done then. I'd

turned the gun down to put the priming in the pan. Well, I was down on my knees. I just squatted down thataway, took deliberate aim at him, and shot. I knowed it had to be a dead shot, or me catched—one or another.

"*Spang* said the rifle, and at the crack of the gun the bear dashed. And I rise and took right after him. Now there was a chase, shore as you're living. Well, it was about a hunderd yards, I reckon, to the swamp on the other side. I made a brave run that far. I thought I'd see him fall any minute, and I wanted to see that sight.

"So when he landed into the bushes, I stopped. I reckon I was about thirty steps behind him. The next thing occurred to my mind was to get out of that place. . . . So you better know I was making all the railroad time I could. I know it wasn't so, but I'm going to tell you: I could hear that bear come a-sousing [in the bay] right in behind me.

"I've had lots of contests with bears and alligators and things, but that's about as near as I ever come to getting bear-catched.

"That was my initiation, and it was a pretty bad one too. Like George Stokes said that time he got catched in the storm, with the timber falling all about him, I wouldn't given *ten cents* for my chances."

Bears were not the only animals worthy of a tale. Uncle Allen recalled these deer stories as well.

The Buck Fight

"I see two old buck hitch and fight one time, to see which one was the best man. I was in gunshot of them at the time. I was a-hunting on Black Jack Island, and it was soon one morning. I got up in gunshot of one buck. He raised his head up and looked down the swamp, and I knowed he seed something. There was another buck. He'd come out and was a-watching this one. This one was standing right still. I knowed he couldn't get away without my shooting of him, and I thought I'd watch and wait.

"Well, when he started, he come right on out. And I soon saw he didn't see me. He was looking right at the other one. He come up within, I reckon, ten or fifteen steps of the other one, and he stopped again. The other hadn't moved. He stood right there with his head raised up and his horns a-glittering. They stood still, I reckon, for as much as a minute. All at once, that one that had come out of that point, begun to circle. Started his circle right around him. Went around, I expect, two or three times, and every circle he'd come in closer.

"And he got his circle out, the last circle he made around. I suppose he was within five or six yards. His hair was just turned the wrong way, bristled back. And he got right in front of him, and made a dash *just like that*, and the other one, he catched him. I thought I'd see a big scuffle, but I didn't. It happened so quick I couldn't tell, but one whipped, and I don't know which one it was. But there was a popping of horns. The one that run, he done some running, too. He got away from that place.

"The one that was left, he stood there looking after him, *just thataway*. And I got him to running. I put a ball right through him. He run, I reckon, fifteen or twenty steps, and tumbled right over.

"That happened on Black Jack Island, on a point that's called 'Bee Tree Point,' about three and a half miles from the east end."

The Fawn

"On our first trip to Buck Prairie me and my brother Sam killed two deer the first evening, and we camped in what they call Green-house Camp. Next morning we went up to the prairie, more to look than anything else. Going along we saw a deer feeding, and shot it down. I got out of the boat, and up jumped a fawn. It took the way I'd come in, and I took after it. Now if you've ever seen a lively race, we had it— me and the fawn. I run it out in the prairie, I reckon, as far as the gate yonder. I overhauled it and brought it back to the boat.

"Next day started to bring the fawn home. Heerd the water sloshing across the prairie. It was four old bucks. We kept right on till we killed the last one—all four of 'em. So we had eight deer and our dog along with us, and our trumpery, all in one boat. Now we had a *load*. Gone three days from home.

"Had that fawn in a crucus sack with his head stuck out. When we got home and let him out, he was just as gentle. They're an easy thing to gentle. He growed till he got to be a right good deer. We had him in hyere a year or two. Dogs wouldn't bother him; they were used to him. He wouldn't bother the corn, but if you had a garden, he'd tear that up."

Once in the piney woods of Chessers Island on a June day, I had the rare fortune to stumble upon a soft-shelled turtle in the act of depositing its eggs. This distinctly aquatic species comes upon the land at this season, finds a patch of soft ground, excavates a hole with its hind feet, lays its complement of eggs therein, carefully fills up the hole with earth, and makes for its home in the water once more. But after going a few yards, it pauses to scratch up the ground vigorously, scattering the earth about and so leaving a conspicuous trace of its presence. This shrewd act, known to the Okefinokee hunters as "scuffling," naturally tends to draw the attention of marauding animals away from the exact spot where the eggs have been concealed. When I related my observation to Uncle Allen, he had some comments of his own to add.

Turtle Ways

"Yes, sir, they've got that knowledge. They're given that knowledge, or they wouldn't do it. Everything according to its time or its manner. He wants to deceive whatever hunts the eggs; he don't want the eggs found. That's his mode. Them yaller-bellied tarrapins [Florida terrapins], they just lay their eggs anywhere. Don't scuffle a-tall. Gophers [gopher turtles] the same way. The old soft-shell turtle is given sense. It's a sharp trick. One wouldn't catch on to it.

"In the first outset, when they come out, they locate a place where they want to dig their hole. And they ain't like everything else. If I was going to dig a hole, I'd use my fore feet. But he digs with his hind feet. He takes one handful of dirt at a throw and throws it out *thataway*. Then he'll change and throw it out the other way. He gets his hole dug and lays his eggs, then kivers 'em with his hind feet. Then he starts off.

"Come to the scuffling part now. He won't start to scuffle till he gets off ten or twelve feet. Then starts scuffling. Keeps moving along and scuffling. Then he'll stop that and go on to his home again in the water. I suppose he does that to save his eggs, to fool them that wants to eat 'em. I know it fooled me, till I got catched on to

it. Lots-a-times they bury themselves before they go to the water and stay there ten or twelve hours.

"I seed a sight of them things one evening, just like a bunch of sheep. You could see them things, a dozen or two in a bunch, just a drift. It was a dry time. I seed them things a-feeding all over the prairie. It looked like they was feeding on grass, to the best of my judgment. It was in the summer season. They eat fish, and crawfish, and things like that. When I find where a turtle has scuffled, I don't dig for the eggs. I take me a stick and find the hole.

"The jackdaw [fish crow], the raccoon, and the bear will eat the eggs. They sure love a egg. They're drilled to it. They go right to the place. They know where it is. The jackdaw will sit around while the turtle's at work; wait on him; fight up in the tree with each other—reckon they are all hungry and all want to get there first. Coon, he small feller, digs a small hole [to get the eggs]. But the bear, with his paws he'll dig a hole. The old gip [female dog] finds pups [gives birth], and will be hungry and range these woods, digging turtle eggs."

"I could keep you writing a week or two," continued Uncle Allen. "I've been in many places in the Okefinokee—seen many things."

One day while we were talking about reptiles, he told me of an astounding episode involving one reptile whose size and habits lend it distinction above all others in the swamp. There is also a melancholy interest in the present story, for such a sight as Allen Chesser here described never again will be witnessed in our day.

Years before I knew him, other lifelong residents of the swamp had told me how it used to seem that one could walk across an

Okefinokee lake on 'gator backs. So the abundance reported here is readily comprehensible. It was before the days when hide-hunters had so greatly reduced the ranks of this interesting saurian. Later in the season I visited the exact scene of the story and saw how accurately the spot had been described.

Even within the ten years before Uncle Allen told this story, he and a companion killed fifty-eight alligators in a single night on Buzzard Roost Lake, which is scarcely a quarter of a mile in its greatest diameter.

A Sight of Alligators

"Now I want to tell you about a sight of alligators I seed one time. I'm satisfied there ain't many people willing to believe such a story as that, but it's true.

"That occurred at the Buzzard Roost Lake. Hyere's the lake [scratching a diagram on the ground], and hyere's a little run [channel] goes out about thirty yards broad. And right hyere at the end is a little round lake. These alligators, I suppose, they must-a-driv all the fish out of this big lake and down this road [the outlet]. It was in between daylight and sunrise. I heerd the racket before I got there. Me and my brother Sam was together.

"I reckon there was five or six hunderd birds around the edge of that lake—scoggins [herons], blue and white ones, and all kinds.

"We heerd the racket and moved on cautiously. We didn't know what it meant, but we could hear the water just a-churning. Our business was to go a-hunting on Number One Island, and that was the only way we could go. We got in sight and there was a sight to look at. I never seed such a sight before in my life.

"The birds, preachers [great blue herons], they're a powerful shy bird. They cared nothing a-tall for us. Run out boat right in the edge of the lake. The alligators cared nothing for us. There must have been three hunderd of 'em. They'd catch fish that long [a foot and a half]. If they'd catch a perch, you'd hear him fluttering in their mouth— thrr—just like a-that. And the funny part, there'd be a 'gator sometimes that high [a yard] out of the water, and another one on to his tail. He'd think it was a fish.

"When he'd catch a fish, just stick his head up thataway, and another one trying to get it away from him. They'd go right under our boat. Wouldn't pay no attention to us. We stayed there till the sun was about an hour high.

"We fell to shooting, and it was either fourteen or sixteen we killed before they took any notice a-tall. And when they did take a notion to get away, there was a sight to look at—when they commenced smelling the blood. They started down that road. They was that thick. I could-a-walked down that road on 'gator heads. My brother up yonder'll identify to it. It's true.

"We went on then; they give us space. The scoggins, when the 'gators begun to leave, they left too. They was there—from salt-water cranes [wood ibises] right down to little fellers. They picked up the fish around the edge. Them 'gators had the little fish run out, and they'd lodge around the edge.

"Whenever one 'gator would freeze on to another one's tail, it was a sight. He'd jump plumb out of the water.

"Everything was agitated that morning— the birds and the alligators, and even I was amused.

"There must-a-been five hunderd of the birds. Even the injun pullet [green heron] was there, a-gitting his mess."

POTIONS, PORTENTS, BALLADS, AND TALES

This is the second best way to learn about the life and lore of the Okefinokee. Ideally we could roll back time and live among the swampers, for they reveal themselves as they are in the field and on the hunt. They are most natural when they sit around the kitchen table at mealtime or relax on the front porch before bedtime. Francis Harper's notebooks are the next best thing to being there.

While participating daily in Okefinokee culture, Harper had the good sense to preserve some of it. We can hear the delightful tale about how the hoorah bush got its name. We learn the art of forecasting not only the weather but the outcome of a courtship. We mull over dubious potions and cures, and we ponder portents of darker mysteries. We learn the art of hunting from one of the swamp's greatest hunters. And, in typical Okefinokee fashion, we end with song.

SWAMP LORE

How the Hoorah Bush Got Its Name

The hoorah bush (*Pieris nitida*) is one of the swamp's most familiar shrubs. Will Cox related this story of how it received its peculiar name.

"Seems the honey bees had the nectar market all cornered up. They had a complete monopoly. Now the small insects could not stand up to the big bees who got all the honey from the big blossoms. So the Good Lord made a bush with flowers on it that were too little for the big bees to light on. Then the small insects shouted: 'hoorah!' And since that time, this bush has been called the 'hoorah bush.' But the big bees weren't through yet. They crossed up with the fireflies so they could work day and night shifts!"

How a Boy Can Tell If a Girl Loves Him

"We just gather a handful of love vine [*Cuscuta compacta*, an epiphyte] and locate us a bunch of bushes to put it on. Then we take it in our hands and take it around over our heads, throw it and let it lodge on those bushes. Then we name it a girl like we want to. If it lives, we figger she loves us. If it dies, we figger she don't. We take it thisaway around our head and throw it and not look back at the present time. We come back later on to see if it's died or lives"—Lang Johns.

How to Stop Owls from Scaring You

According to Jack Mizell and Arthur Hickox, a "scrich owl" will stop making its dreadful noise if you pull your pocket inside out. Jack added that the "freeze owl" will not holler anymore if someone throws salt in a fire. The Chessers had another remedy: hook your pointing fingers together and pull each hand as hard as you can without breaking the hooked fingers.

A Good Luck Omen

On July 13, 1931 Hamp and I greeted fellow fishermen Jim Mixon and Jim Lloyd. Hamp remarked to me: "Well, the boogerman won't catch us today. We got two Jims on the lake." Later in the day, Aunt Rhodie explained that when two people of the same first name are in a house, you can rest assured that the "haints will be kept off."

How to Know If a Tree Will Be Good for Splitting

"If a tree twists against the sun, you'll just as well leave it. It won't split. If it twists with the sun, it'll split good"—Lone Thrift.

How to Forecast the Weather

"Whenever you go out about suppertime, and it lightnings due north, it's gwine to rain. It'll come on you. It'll come on your place. . . . Now a morning rain is maybe like an old lady's dance—it's quick over"—Lone Thrift.

"Look at the first twelve days of January. Each one of them stands for a month. You judge the weather of the following months by the weather in those days. In the 'Old Twelve Days,' the maple blooms, and the lizards, flies, and other animals come out. Hardly ever are two of those days alike"—Hamp Mizell.

STORIES OF THE CONJURE DOCTOR

[When Hamp Mizell first met Ben Yarborough in the late 1890s, Ben was already in his middle eighties. Ben's sons were singers and fiddlers who taught Hamp some of his first ballads. The Yarboroughs lived near Moniac, Georgia, on the headwaters of the St. Marys River. They knew the Mizells through the Primitive Baptist churches, which brought them together for associa-tion meetings and conferences. Hamp said that "when old Ben was eighty-five, he could dance and sing songs just as lively as his sons. Chewed tobacco all his life, and lived to ninety-six." Like Dan'l Spikes, Ben became something of a local legend. Hamp related the following stories about Ben Yarborough's "conjuring" powers.]

"Old Ben Yarborough was a conjure doctor. And Pink Raulerson's cattle got to where he couldn't pen 'em. Wouldn't go in the pen a-tall. So he sent for Yarborough to see what the trouble was. And he went and spent the night with him. So the next morning, before day, he woke up, waked up Pink Raulerson, told him to take his gun and go down to the northeast corner of the fence. And told him to shoot whatever he found setting on the mouth of the gopher hole. Raulerson denied there being any gopher hole at the corner. But went according to Yarborough's instructions. And there he found a gopher hole. Rabbit setting on the mouth of the hole. He shot the rabbit. His cattle were never any more trouble to pen."

"The first thing I ever see Ben Yarborough do: The hog was down on its back; couldn't stand up. Had been that way for a week. Had been dragging its leg around. He just went out and spit on the hog, motioned his hands around a few times. The hog got right up and walked off. Was perfectly all right. Lived for two years, I know, after that."

"Father had a team of oxens. They'd gone astray in the woods, and he couldn't find 'em. He'd hunted 'em for a week, I reckon.

"Old man Ben told father not to hunt 'em anymore. They'd come home tomorrow evening. That was on a Saturday, and he told him they'd come home Sunday, and come on a run.

"They were setting on the front porch on Sunday, looking down the road. It was about three o'clock in the evening. Well, them oxens come around the head of the branch and run into the road, every one with his tail up, and run right on up to the house, like they'd been in a jacket's nest."

Hamp never could quite figure out one of Uncle Ben's conjure tricks—sending a "telegram" to find out how a sick person was getting along. Back in the 1890s a crew of men operated a dredging rig on the Suwannee Canal, far off in the swamp. The story goes that Ben would roll back his left sleeve, extend his bare arm in the direction of a sick person, and rub the arm with his right fingers till the vein swelled up to the size of Hamp's finger. Then Ben would relay a message about the condition of the sick person, all the while observing his left arm with set jaws and solemn face.

Hamp recalled, "Why, he'd find which direction the sick person lived in and point his hand and fingers in that direction. And he'd rub on the flat side of his arm—he'd have the flat side of his arm up. And a few minutes after he commenced to rub, a big vein would strut up right down the full length of his arm. Then he'd wet the tip of the middle finger. Then he'd commence to touch about on this vein with the tip of his finger.

"And everywhere he'd touch would draw a knot—about as big as a buckshot—right on the vein. And that knot would beat just like a pulse—you could see it beat. Then he'd let it beat for about ten minutes. Then he would tell you how the sick folks was that he was telegramming to."

After Hamp told me about this unusual feat, his sister Rhoda told how "a lot of boys working on that Suwannee Canal would give him a dollar. He'd tell your fortune or what girl you was going to marry."

"Uncle Ben had a beazlestone, just a little rock he had in his pocket. Lay it on you and make it sweat."

Hamp said his father did not believe in paying anyone for "conjure" services. But Ben "didn't charge you anything. . . . If you gave him anything, though, he'd make you a dollar for every cent you give him!"

How to Run the Devil Out of His Den

Lone Thrift recited the following procedure for dealing with an unwanted visitor.

"You can take a gum or a hollow cypress that's pretty thin on the side, about twenty inches long. And you work it off sort of thin. That makes it sound. You put a head over it out of rawhide. Have it wet to put it on, and when it dries, that makes it right like a banjo, don't you know? That makes a sound to it. You put a cord in it, right in the center—a small cord with a knot at one end, so it won't slip out. Take ordinary beeswax and wax the cord. You can take that thing at night, you know, and strip the cord like this with your finger and make *woop-woop-woop*! And bury the open end of the gum in the ground, and strip the cord with your finger. That'd run the devil out of his den, or anything else. And you want to see a man get his hat and gone? He'll leave his hat.

"I can tell you another thing you can do. You know how I could break up the fishing on the lake? You can take a barrel and pull it down head first—open end down, don't you see the point? And tie it to something down there, under the water. You hear somebody coming, and you ease under it and play a piece on it. You start in on that, and business'll pick up. They'll leave here right now. . . . It makes a terrible fuss."

Secrets of the Hunt

The residents of Billys Island were known for their hunting ability and for their obser- vation of various natural signs related to the art. They noticed in particular the position of the moon and the calls of birds. They scarcely would consider hunting except when it was "feed-time."

Jackson Lee noted, "The surest way to tell when it's feed-time is to know where the moon is. Whenever the moon's right straight overhead [south], they feed. Or when it rises or goes down, that's good feed-time. Deer and rabbits, they're the same way. You can tell whether it's feed- time if you kill a rabbit and split him and see his entrails just a-working. When the moon goes to rise or set, or is south, then's the time they feed. Make no difference whether it's daytime or night or what time of day it is. Right late this evening, just be- fore night, would be a good time. The moon'll rise, I expect, just before dark."

David Lee said the calls of certain birds, such as the hooting of the "deer owl," sig- nify feed-time for the animals, and even the fish were thought to bite better at such a time. Likewise, the chattering or fuss of "sapsuckers" or "great-god woodpeckers" (pileated woodpeckers) indicate feed-time. On the eastern side of the swamp, however, the hunters disregarded such matters as the position of the moon or the calls of birds.

The deer naturally figures in the folklore of the swamp. Farley Lee contributed an in- teresting note on the subject. He said the name of "deer owl" is applied locally to the barred owl "because when it hollers, it's feed-time for the deer. A deer may be rest- ing, but when he hears the owl hoot, he gets up or moves about and feeds. So all the old deer-hunters say." Harrison Lee added that when the owl gives its *hoo-ah* note, it means that feed-time is about over.

Another curiosity of the hunt is the sto- ries of white deer. Sam Mizell claimed that Walter Davis killed a white deer below

Folkston. Local tradition has it that this special deer carries a "beazlestone" in its throat. Sometimes coughed up by a deer after it is wounded, the beazlestone has been collected by several hunters. Allen Chesser spoke of seeing them. He said they "grow in the deer's runnet, right where his swaller [esophagus] goes into his maw [stomach]." Farley Lee had a different explanation. He asked if I knew what small object he was wearing about his neck. Confessing that I did not, I asked for an explanation. Farley replied: "Well, sir, it's a bone from the heart of a deer. It's good for heart trouble. My heart used to be might bad, but since I been a-wearing this hyere, it's been a heap better. Once I asked a doctor about it, and he said he didn't doubt it did me good." Other residents of Billys Island have maintained that many deer, not just white ones, have "beazlestones" in or near the heart. (Peter Freuchen's report on *Mammals of Fifth Thule Expedition* (1935) noted this fascinating parallel among the Eskimos: "In the musk-ox there is a bone near the heart to support the vessels. This *os cordis* is worn by some Eskimos as an amulet.")

How to Cure Venison

A generation ago, while deer were amazingly plentiful, though unprotected, Allen and Sam Chesser killed 144 of them in a single year. "Black Jack Island was covered with 'em," Uncle Allen said. "We'd scarcely ever go there without bringing back six or eight. We brought the meat home, salted it, dried it. I can say one thing: I was raised on it. Nowadays I don't get any of it, and it goes hard on me. The boys [sons and nephews] won't get it from

one year's end to the other. I ain't eat a piece of venison since the Lord knows when.

"How do you cure venison? Salt it down, from one day to another, then put it out in the sun for three or four hours. Sometimes there'd be a fuzz a inch long all over a piece of meat. Take it and scrape that off, boil it, and then not cut it, but pull it apart and throw it in the frying pan. Now you'll have to hide your tongue! And you eat a good baked yam with it. In them days I hardly ever eat a mess in there [the kitchen] without a good piece of back-strop."

How to Make Everlasting Shoelaces

The flesh of the fox squirrel (*Sciurus niger*) is much esteemed by the swampers. The dressed hides are prized for their durability, and squirrel hide was used to make shoelaces, pieces of harness, "whip-crackers," and the like. Sam Chesser, pointing to his shoelaces, remarked: "Now there's one of the best dressed leathers I know of—fox squirrel. You can go into the water or the dew with 'em, and they won't never get hard. They're sure an endurable leather. They'll outlast two pair of shoes."

Sam's brother, Allen, explained how the hide was dressed: "Put it to soak in water for three or four days or a week. Then take it out and grain the hair off of it, and the fat off the inside. Boil you some beef brains, and put the hide in them to soak, and leave it there for two or three hours, more or less, till it takes. Then take it out, pull it around, and stretch it till it's dry. It's done then. If you ever lay it down and not stretch it, it's hard. You can dress a deer hide the same way."

Wart Cures

Roxie Chesser had a lot of warts on her hands and feet. Someone told her to cure them this way: "Take as many grains of corn as you have warts. Tie them in a rag, carry them off, and throw them down where someone else will pick them up." Well, one day, on the way to the church meeting at Sardis Church, she carried along the grains and threw them down on the other side of Starling Branch. That very same day Dock Rider came along, picked them up, and carried them back to the Chessers' homeplace. But, true to the cure, Roxie's warts soon went away.

Roxie's husband, W. E. Renshaw, said that a Mr. Crews would take warts off a cow by finding a rotten piece of pine; then he would hit the animal across the back of its neck so that the piece broke and fell on each side of it. While performing the feat, he shouted: "Go away, warts!" He said the warts went away.

Aunt Rhoda Mizell Spaulding had three favorite cures. First: "Slip over to your neighbor's house and steal a dish and rub it on your warts. Then throw it away, and your warts will go away." Second: "You go and take one of them old cow bones in the woods after it's turned white, and you just rub the wart with it, and just place it right back as nigh as you can. And go away and don't look back now. And that'll make the wart go away." Third: "You have some warts on your hand, and you go sell 'em to somebody. Maybe they'll give you a penny or a nickel. Then they'll go away."

Hamp Mizell has done a great business in removing warts by rubbing them until they are soft. Then he blows on them to cool them. After that the warts "shed off" rapidly. Another one of Hamp's cures is to bleed the wart; then put the blood on a grain of corn and give the corn to a chicken.

For Jaundice

Hamp also said you can make a fairly delicious drink for this ailment by placing cherry bark in a bottle and pouring whiskey over it. Another cure for "yellow" jaundice is admittedly an "old fogeyism," said Hamp: "You boil an egg and go out and hunt up one of these big red ant-hills. Then set down by the ant-hill. Eat all the white of the egg and give the yellow to the ants. That's one way they cure the jaunders."

For Stuttering

Jackson Lee said that when he was a small boy, he stuttered so badly that he "couldn't hardly talk." He ate some mockingbird eggs, and, as custom had predicted, he soon talked normally.

Potions for Other Ailments

The potions that follow were copied from an old notebook found on Chessers Island. Like Aunt Rhodie's potions, some contain ingredients that may well do more harm than good.

For Female Trouble
4 tablespoonsful of pot iron
4 tablespoonsful of ginger

4 tablespoonsful of poplar bark
4 tablespoonsful of corncob ashes
4 tablespoonsful of country early (?)
2 tablespoonsful of gun powder

To be pounded together. Take what will lie on the point of a case knife 3 times a day before meals. Danger during pregnancy, and must not be used then.

For Sore Eyes
Mix up clay and hold it over eyes for one hour.

For Itch
Mix kerosene and table salt well. Rub skin well.

For Shingles
Poplar bark
Tallow
Beeswax
Camphor
New turpentine
Tar
Hog lard
Beef foot oil

Use equal parts of each, boiled to a stiff salve. Spread over cloth, and bind to the affected area.

For Gravel Stones
2 ounces sweet lavender
2 ounces Sprits Ninter
2 ounces Balsom compound
1 ounce Laudalum
1 ounce Turpentine

Put all together and shake well. Take one teaspoon full 3 times a day.

For Building a Run Down System
1 tablespoon of dogwood bark
1 tablespoon of cherry bark
1 tablespoon of ginger
1 teaspoon of cinders
1 teaspoon of saltpeter
1 teaspoon of rhubarb

Compound all and run through a sifter. Mix with honey and take what will lie on the point of a case knife, 3 times a day.

BALLADS AND THEIR MAKERS

"Dan'l Spikes" is a Civil War ballad that Allen and Sam Chesser recited to me in August 1922. They were the sons of the composer, William Tennyson Chesser. At the time they introduced me to this legendary character, they were both well past the three-score mark. Spikes had been well known, living on the eastern border of the swamp a few miles north of Chessers Island. He was reputed to be the laziest man in Charlton County. "Too lazy to work, and too lazy to talk," they said, "but a powerful eater."

This ballad used to be recited in a sort of singsong tune. At the time I transcribed it, the refrain was entirely unfamiliar. At a considerably later date I found out that it was a well-known refrain of old English ballads—"derry down." W. T. Chesser, like many folk musicians before him, had borrowed a familiar refrain for his ballad. It would be of little use to search for a printed book of ballads or poetry among the people with whom songs such as this one originated. This is probably the first time "Dan'l Spikes" has been committed to writing.

Unfortunately several additional stanzas could not be recalled by sons of the composer, and these are irretrievably lost.

Daniel Spikes

Come all you good people and listen awhile,
I will sing you a ditty that will cause you to
 smile
About old Dan'l Spikes, he lived very near.
He cropped it for his mother this ensuing year.

Refrain, repeated after each stanza:
    Derry down,
    Derry down, derry down.
    It was always too wet or too dry for to
     plough.
    And as for the hoe, he worked little with
     that,
    As for the hoe, he worked little with that.

Dan'l Spikes stole a hog, as we have heard
 said.
And he'll steal another, we know very well.
Behind people's backs he will steal all,
And come to their faces, he'll steal nothing at
 all.

There's one thing more I want to tell you now:
He was charged with the killing Miz Chancy's
 sow.
I do suppose the thing about right,
For it filled the old gentleman full of fight.

The people around here have proved very kind,
Come to the conclusion Miz Nobles to find
Brooks, Hatcher, an' Chesser an' other good
 friends
Had added to her needs like charitable men. *

Old Dan'l Spikes, he happened to get the hang
 [the news],
Put on his old coat, and went battling his
 hams. †
He went to Miz Unity's, and there took a seat,
Waiting for a bite of old Hatcher's beef.

Now just after dinner he begun to feel worse.
He was throbbing and beating and just fit to
 burst.
He looked like a man, three days he'd been
 dead.
He crawled off so softly and went to bed.

["Dan'l Spikes" makes fun of an Okefinokee character who resisted service in the Confederate cause. He was ridiculed with the most effective weapon—sarcasm. But what of those who deserted? Some young men, as we know, fled the battlefields for the protection of the swamp. Even though residents were not slaveholders, many volunteered to serve the cause of Johnny Reb. The "Okefinokee Rifles" and other units drawn from southern Georgia included on their rosters the names of volunteers from the Mizell, Chesser, and other swamp families. These same families, however, were sympathetic toward the deserter, even though this song passed along by Mattie Chesser laments the error of his ways.]

Young Soldier Boy

Young soldier boy, a warning take,
And never promise and forsake
And never from your colors fly
Unless you see you're doomed to die.

---

* As Sam Chesser related, "In Civil War times the women left at home were looked after, to get something to eat. There were men appointed for that bizness." So Brooks, Hatcher, and (W. T.) Chesser constituted the local committee. The "Miz Nobles" of this stanza and "Miss Unity" of the next are the same person—Mrs. Unity Nobles.
† This is a picture of coat-tails flapping: "Had a ol' long coat, come way down hyere to his shoe quarters," Allen Chesser explained. In another part of the swamp I have heard this garment called a "ham-knocker coat."

I had a sweetheart low did lie;
She sent for me to see her die.
I asked my captain for a furlough;
The answer was I could not go.

Some friends told me to wait and see,
Perhaps some day I may be free.
And on my heart that promise did lie,
And from my colors I did fly.

From January till July,
On rocks and boards how could I lie?
And those young soldiers unkind to me
In time of my calamity.

They led me to the garden green,
And such a sight I never had seen.
My days was past, my race was run,
I saw those soldiers load their guns.

They led me to the very place
And pulled my cap down o'er my face.
My days was past, my race was run,
My life was ended by those guns.

I had no friends to take my part
Nor see those balls that pierced my heart,
No one to weep, no one to pray,
But remember me on a dying day.

When I am gone would you sing this song
And think of me when I am gone.
Remember too the soldier boy
A sweetheart and a mother's joy.

[The young girls on Chessers Island knew the song as "Little Mohee," but others in the swamp agreed with Sarah Martin Thrift that the title is "The Lassie Mohee." The version that is printed below was sung to Francis Harper by Gertie Lou and Ruby Chesser and was transcribed by Joan Moser. Like many familiar ballads, this one circulated quite early in printed form in America, and most versions agree on basic details. Scholars of the ballad disagree about the origin of this one: some say it is a British broadside; others argue that it came from the South Seas. Perhaps the most interesting adaptation is called "The Creole Girl," set in the swamps of Pontchartrain of Louisiana; here a man wandering in the region is befriended by a Creole maid who refuses to marry him, because her lover is at sea.

The song has special significance for the Okefinokee, because one of the earliest recorded myths from the region concerns hunters who were lost in the swamp. As Bartram recorded the story, these men met "a company of beautiful women, whom they called daughters of the sun." Upon returning to civilization, the hunters repeated the stories about these fascinating creatures to their countrymen, who "were enflamed with an irresistible desire to invade, and make conquest of, so charming a country."]

Little Mohee

1. As I was out walk-ing for pleasure one day, In
sweet re-cre-- a--tion to while time a--way.

2. As I sat amusing myself on the grass,
   Whom should I spy but a fair Indian lass.

3. She sat down beside me and taking my hand,
   Says you are a stranger, and in a strange land.

4. But if you will follow you're welcome to come,
   And dwell in the cottage that I call my home.

5. The sun was just sinking far over the sea,
   When I wandered along with my pretty Mohee.

6. Together did wander, together did rove,
   'Til we came to the cottage in the coconut grove.

7. And these kind expressions she made unto me,
   If you will consent, sir, to stay here with me,

8. And go no more roving upon the salt sea,
   I'll teach you the language of the Lassie Mohee.

9. O, no, my dear maiden, that never can be,
   For I have a true love in my own country.

10. And I'll not forsake her for I know she loves me,
    And my heart is as true as the pretty Mohee.

11. It was early one morning, one morning in May,
    When to this fair maiden these words I did say,

12. I have to leave you so farewell my dear,
    My ship's sails are spreading and home I must steer.

13. The last time I saw her she stood on the strand,
    And as my boat passed her she waved me her hand,

14. Saying, when you have landed with the girl that you love,
    Think of your little Mohee in the coconut grove,

15. And when I had landed upon my native shore,
    With friends and relations around me once more,

16. I gazed all about me, no one could I find,
    That's fit to compare with the pretty Mohee.

17. The girl I had trusted proved untrue to me,
    I'll turn my course backward upon the salt sea.

18. I'll turn my course backward far over the sea,
    I'll go spend my days with my pretty Mohee.

[Folksongs long have been recognized for their educational value, and these favorites from Chessers Island are no exception. The patriarch William Tennyson Chesser, who settled Chessers Island before the Civil War, was a reader of books and valued education. He encouraged his children to learn and to read. Since Mr. Chesser found it easy to make songs and ballads, it is likely that he was the author of these variations of traditional songs. In typical Chesser fashion, each piece rides smoothly over an undercurrent of humor.]

The Alphabet Song

A was an archer. He shot a frog.
B was a butcher. He butchered a dog.
C was a comer. He come in apace.
D was a drunkard. He was red in the face.
E was a eater. Eat all of his peas.
F was a fiddler. He fiddled on his knees.
G was a jointer. He joined in a house.
H was a hunter. He hunted a mouse.
I was an Ireland man. He followed the Pope.
J was a Judas. He betrayed all.
K was a knave. With his neck in a rope.
L was a liar. He told lies.
M was a miller. He ground flies.
N was a knower. He knowed all.
O was a officer. Round as a ball.
P was a peddler. He sold pins.

Q was a quarreller. He broke shins.
R was a runner. He run races.
S was a seamstress. She sewed laces.
T was a turner. He turned top
.   .   .   .   .   .

W was a whittler. He whittled the top.

Backwards from Ten

Ten guinea pigs in the rye field a-rooting.
Nine gray geese in the green field a-grazing.
Eight parsons in the pulpit a-preaching.
Seven flat flying ficating fish sailing in sailing
    boats from Madagasco to the end of
    Geneva.
Six Injun monkeys dressed in green and gray
    clothing, going hand-in-hand up the
    mountain.
Five thornless thayers.
Four headless pears.
Three plump partridges.
Two pidgeon cherry trees.
A knife for the oracle!

The two songs that follow are also a part of the Chessers Island song bag. The first was sung by Gertie Lou and Ruby Chesser. The second was learned many years ago from Mrs. Allen Chesser by her daughter Mrs. Walter Renshaw and her granddaughter Nina Renshaw.

Sailor on the Deep Blue Sea

1. It was on a Sun- day ev- ning, Just a-
'bout the hour- of three, When my dar-lin' star-ted t'
leave me, To sail - on the deep blue sea.

2. He promised to write me a letter,
   He promised to write to me,
   But I haven't heard from my darlin',
   Since he sailed on the deep blue sea.

3. My mother's dead and buried,
   My father's forsaken me,
   And I have no one to love me,
   But the sailor on the deep blue sea.

4. O, captain, can you tell me,
   Can you tell me where he may be,
   O, yes, my little maiden
   He's drown-ded in the deep blue sea.

5. Farewell to friends and relations,
   This is the last you'll see of me,
   For I'm goin' to end my troubles
   By drown-ding in the deep blue sea.

[Hamp Mizell, a walking library of swamp lore, specialized in fiddle songs. He delighted in clever rhymes, especially in those bordering on the nonsensical. Once Hamp started to recite these brief songs, Francis Harper discovered, there was no way to stop him short of a dozen or so at one sitting. Here are some of Hamp's favorites.]

"The Best Man in Charlton County"

"Back in the nineties, John ——— was supposed to be physically the best man in Charlton County up to that time. They were eating at the breakfast table. And there was some remark about John being the best man in the county physically. And

Higher Up the Cherry Tree

1. High-er up the cher-ry tree, the ri-per grows the ber-ries. The more you court a pre-tty fair miss, the soon-er she will marry.

2. Don't court you one with a rovin' eye,
   Nor one with too much money,
   Court you one with two blue eyes,
   Kiss her and call her honey.

Fred ———— made some remarks that he wasn't so sure of that. So after breakfast they got out on the new piece of road they had there to try it out. And they got Uncle Rob Mizell to set on a nail keg to play the fiddle for them to fight.

"So Fred whooped John—that is, beat him down to where he couldn't do nothing. He never did say he was whooped. He never would acknowledge he'd been whooped. Fred from then on bore the name of being the best man in the county physically, till he died." This is the song that Uncle Rob fiddled on that fateful day.

Abraham and Isaac went out for a fight,
And Abraham bound for to smash him.
He picked up a brick, and hit him such a lick,
He knocked him on the other side of Jerdan.

Hawk built a nest in the top of the pine,
The old gray goose in the garden.
The duck built a nest at the foot of the bridge,
And the jay on the other side of Jerdan

Had an old gobbler, had but one feather in his
    wing.
Just one feather, I'm mighty certain.
Lift up the lid for to put him in the pot,
And he boggled on the other side of Jerdan.

Chorus:
    Roll up your sleeves, boys,
    Say what you please,
    Jerdan's a hard road to travel, I believe.

Hauling Corn

"We used to sing this song at Hopkins [a
logging settlement]. The boys got so rough,
boss Harry Quarterman moved 'em to a
shanty where they could sing and dance.
The boys made up the chorus, because Harry told 'em it sounded like hauling corn and
throwing it in the crib."

Mary had a little lamb
Born on Christmas day.
She picked him up and spanked him good,
And named him Henry Clay.

Neighbor, lend your mule today.
I'll lend you mine tomorrow.
I bought my mule to ride myself.
I neither lend nor borrow.

Chorus:
    Hauling corn, hauling corn,
    Keep my wagon a-hauling corn.

Rock, Rock, My Little Love

Went to see my little love,
Something new to tell her.

She need not depend on me no longer,
She can hunt another feller.

Chorus:
    Rock, rock, my little love,
    Rock, rock, I say.

Peafowl crow for the middle of the night,
And the Shanghai crow for day.
Anybody going to see my girl
Better be getting away.

Going to see my little love,
Tell her if you please.
Before she goes to roll her bread,
To roll her dirty sleeves.

Hamp said the first song he heard when
he was a little boy was this one. The original singer, he guessed, was Nathan Dixon
of Charlton County. The song probably
originated on Cornhouse Creek.

The Rabbit Song

Where you going, little rabbit,
Where you going, I say?

Ain't got time to tell you,
There's a little dog on the way.

Rabbit, rabbit, you hear them dogs?
Yes, but I'm making for a holler log.

Rabbit, rabbit, your ears mighty long.
Yes, my gracious, they're sot on wrong.

Rabbit, rabbit, your foot mighty round.
Yes, my gracious, I can put it on the ground.

Chorus:
    Ain't you getting there, rabbit,
    Ain't you getting there now?
    My gracious, rabbit, ain't you getting there
        now?

The Doctor Who Fiddled

Dr. A. C. Dorminy of Hoboken, in Brantley County, Georgia, was an old friend of Hamp Mizell's. The two were drawn together by a common love of fiddling and folk singing. He was in the habit of making occasional visits to Suwannee Lake, where he could indulge fully his enjoyment of old-fashioned music. He had been raised in Pulaski County, about 100 miles northwest of the Okefinokee, in the Lime-sink region of Georgia. I was fortunate in obtaining some interesting information from him about yodeling and about the fauna of his native part of the state. He was probably in his fifties when I met him in 1931. Although apparently an unschooled doctor, he was respected and was consulted by many local residents. Some called him a "horse and buggy" doctor.

While we were on Hamp's shady porch in the late afternoon of July 2, 1931, Doc Dorminy leaned back and sang and played "The Cowhouse Gap" with delight:

Me and my wife
And my wife's pap
Walked all the way
From the Cowhouse Gap

We was away down the road
With a horse that would balk,
And me and my wife
Had to get out and walk.

He had other versions of this song that I did not manage to record. Although I have not been to this gap, I understand that it is an opening or passage in the slough or bay separating the eastern end of Cowhouse Island from the mainland. A road passes through the opening. The Gap O' Grand Prairie, with which I am quite familiar, is a fairly wide boat passage, bordered on each side by a cypress bay and leading from Chessers Prairie to Grand Prairie. A few years ago I saw the song "Cumberland Gap" in a book about the American frontier; this song was sung by west-bound pioneers as they journeyed onward through this gap into Kentucky. I assumed immediately that both "gap" songs were related.

As he began the following song, Aunt Rhoda Mizell Spaulding noted that she knew it also:

All I want in this creation
Is a pretty little wife and a big plantation.

All I want to make me happy
Is two little boys to call me pappy.

One named Pete and the other named Davey.
One eat the sop and other eat the gravy.

Hamp said that his Uncle Rob, like Doc Dorminy, kept a rattlesnake's rattle in his fiddle. Why? To make it sound better, to give it a better tone. Doc Dorminy's father learned to play on a gourd fiddle with a homemade bow: "Had an old gray horse, with a long tail. He went and stole part of that for the bow."

On July 3, 1931, I took some movies of Doc Dorminy fiddling with Hamp collaborating part of the time by beating on the strings with a broomstraw. This practice adds to the volume and enables the dancers at a frolic to keep better time. Hamp held the straw near the end of the strings with his left thumb and forefinger. While Doc played, Hamp struck the strings of the fiddle with the straw, producing a staccato effect and doubling the rhythm. Hamp called this practice "beating a tattoo" or "beating the strings."

Here is a sampling of songs Doc Dorminy played at the frolic:

Oaks grow tall, and pines grow slim.
Rise up there, you cigarette stub,
And choose your partner in.

There was a happy little miller
Who lived by himself.
All the bread and cheese he had,
He laid it on the shelf.

Wouldn't pick cotton
And wouldn't pull hay,
Wouldn't take a whipping,
And wouldn't run away.

Old woman, old woman, (slowly)
What makes you treat me sooooo.
   (plaintively)

I love tater pie,
And I love tater pudding.
Give it all away
To see Sally Goodin.

Going away to Georgia
To see them pretty girls dance.
Johnny come along
With a fiddle and a bow.

If I go to my shack
With a hog on my back,
It's nobody's business but mine

If I get on my bunk,
And drink till I get drunk,
It's nobody's business but mine.

That girl of mine
Wants to ramble all the time,
But it's nobody's business but mine.

Coffee grows on white oak trees,
River flows with brandy.
Go choose you one that'll stand by you,
As sweet as sugar or candy.

Refrain, played three times:
   Two in the middle and you better get about,
   Shoo-lie-lulu, my darling.
   Four in the middle and they kicked two out,
   Shoo-lie-lulu, my darling.

Noah Lee eating huckleberries on Billys Lake. May 1921.

James Henry Lee with a hard-backed cooter on Billys Island. May 1921.

Hamp Mizell and his children at Suwannee Lake. The cypress gate was over fifty years old and had been used at the old Mizell place in Charlton County. Originally it had no sawn lumber in it. May 1930.

Huckleberry pickin' with Maggie Mizell, Aunt Rhodie, and Jean Harper near a cypress pond at Suwannee Lake. July 1931.

Hamp Mizell strumming his homemade banjo. May 1930.

The young men of the Okefinokee sample a famous local recipe. June 1921.

Henry Harrison Lee "sticking his bill" in a 'gator hole on Floyds Island Prairie. June 1921.

A turpentiner at work on Bugaboo Island. June 1929.

A crew of turpentiners with a yoke of small oxen haul firewood and hand-hewn timbers on Bugaboo Island. June 1929.

Lone Thrift and his ox cart. No date.

Picking tobacco in Charlton County. June 1929.

Harry, Mattie, and Mrs. Allen Chesser singing "The Turtle Dove" from The Four Note Book. *April 1933.*

In the "sorup shed" where famous Chessers Island cane syrup has been made for generations, Mattie Chesser stands near the tub and Elma and Elsie Rider tend the syrup kettle. April 1933.

Maggie Mizell grinds corn for the chickens in a "steel mill" at Owen Thrift's. Note Uncle Owen's mud-and-stick chimney. May 1930.

The Chesser family putting fodder out to dry. July 1922.

Uncle Lone Thrift, keeping watch over the Suwannee Lake fishing preserve, is joined by (left to right) *Maggie Mizell, Gertrude Robinson, Alice Mizell, and Rhodie Mizell. April 1932.*

Dave, Farley, Lem, and Jackson Lee setting off on a hunt. December 1916.

Farley and David Lee in camp at Dinner Pond Lake. December 1916.

An Okefinokee otter hunter. His hound was trained upon scenting its prey to jump overboard and to pursue and attack in the water. Hunting otters this way was more effective than trapping. December 1916.

Marion Lee accompanied Francis Harper on a voyage down the St. Marys River. August 1921.

Francis Harper poling across Mud Lake. May 1912.

Mr. and Mrs. W. O. Gibson at their home near Sardis Church. Mr. Gibson was the local "Hardshell" preacher, a former member of the state legislature, and according to Francis Harper "probably the most intelligent man in Charlton County." April 1932.

The Mizell children at play in their front yard at Suwannee Lake. June 1929.

Francis Harper and two Billys Island boys, Noah and Lester Lee. July 1921.

Brooms, bowls, skillets, and other household paraphernalia, most of it homemade, adorn a wall at Ben Chesser's. June 1930.

Black laborers from the logging crew going by flat car from Billys Island to Billys Bay. June 1921.

Hamp Mizell used to say that if he could hear a person talk, he could tell immediately whether the person grew up in the Okefinokee. This brief glossary originated with Hamp's observation. Here, gleaned from the pages of Francis Harper's many notebooks, is a sampling of swamp talk—the rich and colorful expressions of the Okefinokee folk. Some are Old English or Scottish expressions that the sons and daughters of the British Isles who settled here and in the Appalachians preserved and passed on. Others are unique to the Okefinokee.

The language of the swamper was his badge of individuality, and Francis Harper championed both the language and what it represented. He deplored the rapid movement toward "sameness" among Americans and was an unrelenting opponent of unimaginative conformity. He believed that mass communication—the newspaper, radio, motion picture, and television—fostered bland patterns of speaking and, even worse, banal patterns of thinking. And these corrupting forces were given credence, said Harper, by modern educators who too often equate backwoods speech with ignorance.

In some ways Harper's fears that the language would vanish were unfounded. People in southeast Georgia still talk about going on a "progue" for a "passel" of "pinders." Of course, in this part of the "country," it does not take much of a "muzog" before one can "fetch 'em."

addled	Mentally weak or crazy. The term is applied to both people and animals.
affirminant	As Uncle Jesse Aldridge preached, Old Man Martin grunted approval. Aunt Rhoda Spaulding called him the "affirminant."
afyeard	Afraid. "One dog laid by the bear, and the other dogs was afyeard of him"—Lone Thrift.
all in	Exhausted. One or two of the dogs "blowed off," as Ben Chesser put it, toward the end of the hunt, announcing by a mournful note that they were "all in" or tired out.

along an' along	Periodically. Mrs. Allen Chesser often uses this phrase meaning "from time to time."
balance	"They had your balance," Harry Chesser would say, meaning "they've got your number."
bar	Castrated hog, short for "barrow." "Mammy found me an old bar today"—attributed to Dan'l Spikes by Zeke Henderson.
bastard bread	"Frying pan bread is 'bastard bread,' because it is a mixture of flour and cornmeal"—Lang Johns.
batteries	Small swamp islands. "I run on to one of them batteries. It's one of them things covered with broomstraw"—Lone Thrift.
battling stick	A small wooden paddle used by the women of Chessers Island to pound clothes during laundering.
bear drive	Another term for a bear chase in which a person follows a team of dogs in search of a bear.
beating strings	Fiddler's technique. Jack Mizell's wife joined in by "beating the strings" of the violin with a round strip of palmetto.
beazlestone	Perhaps "beazlestone" derives from "bezoar stone," a sixteenth-century term for a knot of animal matter formed around a nucleus of foreign substance. In the Okefinokee the "beazlestone" reputedly had magical healing power. "A deer, white-pieded, or one with streaked hoofs, has a beazlestone [in the stomach?], hard and oily; looks like a brown pullet's egg"—Hamp Mizell.
blowed off	The doleful howl of exhaustion and despair of a dog that has given up after a long and unsuccessful chase.
blowzey	Mrs. Sarah Thrift uses the word "blowzey" to mean untidy, referring to hair or clothes, etc.
blubber	Bubbles. "First thing I knowed, there was blubbers I saw"—Lone Thrift.
blue john	Owen Gibson calls skimmed milk by this name.
blue whistler	Referring to turpentine barrels with a sixty-gallon capacity, Uncle Lone Thrift said, "We call 'em blue whistlers."
boozy	Intoxicated. "He was boozy," Hamp Mizell said in reference to a bothersome person.

branch	A small stream or creek.
biggity	Tense with anger. "He [a bear] was mad. He walked just like a billy goat. You've seen them when they're mad—feel biggity"—Allen Chesser.
bread-tray hump	There were two John Steedleys, one of whom is known as Bear John (from his alleged stealing of hogs), and the other as Bread-tray John because he has a hump on his chest as well as on his back.
calaberment	Describing the loud noise made by an animal, Hamp Mizell said, "You never heard such a calaberment in your life."
catheads	A popular name for biscuits. Also called "owl heads."
chance	Quantity. "Sunday morning, the first thing when we got up, my wife told me what a great chance of chickens she had hatched off"—Lone Thrift.
cheap	Nervous or scared. Uncle Owen Thrift said he felt "mighty cheap" when he thought a bear was going to kill him.
chip box	Small box made of thin wood, used to collect turpentine from the base of pine trees.
chivaree	A serenade by musicians on special occasions, including but not limited to weddings.
choke rag	Neck-tie. "Well, that's the first time I ever see you with a choke rag"—Allen Chesser.
common	Pleasant or likeable. It's considered a compliment to be called a "common" person.
Confederate War	Older swampers, in particular, used this for "Civil War."
conjure	Clairvoyant. Ben Yarborough had the reputation of being able to forecast human and natural events. He was also a "conjure doctor," i.e., he could perform magical healing. At one time Lone Thrift was thought to be a conjurer.
corn wallet	Uncle Owen Thrift had a corn wallet, a pouch he used for carrying corn in when calling up his hogs.
country	Not to be confused with "country" (nation) or "county," this term refers to a region that may cross county lines: "It was the master freshet we ever had in this country"—Lone Thrift.

coursing	Tracking or tracing. "We put in to trace it up—to see which way it [the colony of bees] went. . . . Had 'em to bait, and was coursing all day"—Hamp Mizell.
cow house	A barn for cows or cattle.
crab	Pull. Ben Chesser talking about cows' eating grass says, "They'll crab it off and eat it."
Cracker	A name for swampers, preferred especially by older residents. Jack Mizell referred to himself as "about the last old light'ood knot Cracker in the county that can play a fiddle." Francis Harper used the term "Cracker" to mean "poor white" when he first visited the swamp, but after learning more about the people, he accepted it as a name for most old-line local residents; indeed, eventually he took pride in speaking of himself as a Cracker. In fifteenth- and sixteenth-century England and Scotland the verb *crack* referred to the actions of a noisy, boasting, independent person. The Scotch-Irish who settled the southern frontier were called "Crackers" by the British authorities.
cracklins	Pork skin that has been fried until crisp. Often used as an ingredient in a kind of corn bread.
crawfish	Used as a verb to describe the actions of a devious person. "He crawfished like a dog," Lone Thrift said of a turpentine man who tried to cheat him in a business matter.
croker sack	A burlap bag used for seed; also called "crocus" sack or bag, perhaps because the brand name "Crocus" once could be found on such bags.
cromb	Used as a verb, meaning to catch or kill something, usually an animal, by hooking or hitting it with a stick or implement.
demogra	Possibly an Indian word for "galls" or any kind of infection. "Dave Mizell called galls 'demogra'"—Hamp Mizell.
dew claws	Usually describes a man on his tiptoes: "When Uncle Owen Gibson would get up on his dew claws, when he got to raring [in the middle of a sermon], I'd lose him right now"—Hamp Mizell. Also used to describe alliga-

	tors in the act of mating. Jackson Lee's term for dew claws is "petty hoofs."
dip	Verb used to describe the act of gathering resin from boxes on pine trees. "I knew a certain man to dip six barrels a day"—Lone Thrift.
disremember	Forget. "Now I've seen that twice, Mr. Harper. I disremember where the other was"—Lone Thrift.
do how	Used as a synonym for "what?" Harper notes that this expression had not gone entirely from the region.
done	Used widely for "already," as in "He done did that."
driver	Designates the lead hunter who pursues game, usually with the help of dogs. Ben Chesser says the driver on a bear hunt does a lot of hollering, but not the standers.
dumpling driver	"Adam's apple," the thyroid cartilage at the front of the neck. Also called a "goozling."
evening	Any time between noon and dark. "Me and Nathan Dixon was paddling down the canal, about three o'clock in the evening"—Hamp Mizell.
extortionist	One who exaggerates. "Ransom Steedley was something of an extortionist in telling stories"—Hamp Mizell.
fitified	Possessed by fits of irrational behavior. Little Rhodie told Francis Harper that she had picked up a rattlesnake, and Aunt Sarah made her throw it down, saying she would be "fitified."
fixing	Ready to do something. "And whenever he got there the old bear was just a-fixing to die"—Owen Smith.
fixments	Special tools or instruments, such as Harper's zoological "fixments" or Uncle Lone Thrift's dental "fixments."
flinder	To harass or bother. "If the flies flinders him [the horse], he'll work faster"—Owen Thrift. Also indicates that something is out of order. "A car has gone to flinders what's wrecked and busted to pieces"—Harrison Lee.
flume out	Distraught. Lone Thrift, describing his wife's concern about the hawks that had been destroying her chickens: "Well, she flume out about it."
foot	To walk. Owen Thrift, describing a self-proclaimed strong man: "Boys, I'm the best man ever footed Waresboro."

fram	To thrash. Used primarily by older swampers to describe violent movements of persons or animals. "Dud . . . heard him [the horse] framming in the stall"—Owen Thrift.
fresh, freshet	Used to designate a sudden heavy rain that causes streams to overflow their banks.
frolic	A social occasion at which men and women participate in square dancing to the accompaniment of guitars, fiddles, or banjos.
gallberry child	A child born out of wedlock. Also called a "wood's colt."
get-up	Joke. "When I get on them Injun mounds and stomp my foot, they'll answer, 'nothing.' That's one of Ridley Chesser's get-ups"—Lang Johns.
gip	A female dog.
goozling	Another term for "Adam's apple." Also called a "dumpling driver."
gower	To stare. Used especially by older swampers, meaning "to study something while looking at it."
grabble	To dig or scratch the earth. People "grabble" for potatoes, i.e., remove some potatoes from the root system beneath the earth without killing the plant. Rabbits "grabble" for recently planted corn seed, etc.
hack	To overcome. Lone Thrift, speaking of a grandson's recent illness which had nearly vanished: "They've got it pretty well hacked."
ham-knocker	A coat, worn by a man, which reaches his thighs or "hams." Gator Joe Saunders spoke of Dan'l Spikes's "ham-knocker coat."
Hardshell	A member of the old-line Primitive Baptist church, the dominant religious body in the Okefinokee and in rural south Georgia.
hassle	A term for the panting sound made by animals, used by most hunters of the region.
hip-shooten	Tired out. "Ben Chesser had been opining that he was 'hip shooten'—a new one on me, meaning having given out as to his 'hind legs'"—Francis Harper.
hobbiedehoy	Irresponsible young person. Speaking of a prothonotary

warbler's nest that had been robbed, Hamp Mizell said the culprit could have been a "hobbiedehoy, snake, squirrel, coon, or something."

holders — Canine teeth of dogs. "And it was double-tushed, like these double-tushed dogs. Ain't you seen 'em, with two holders on each side?"—Lone Thrift.

holler — Abdominal cavity. "The alligator was wounded—shot in the holler—and couldn't go in the water"—Lone Thrift.

hollering — A form of yodeling by swampers which can be heard for two or three miles, depending on weather conditions and the skill of the hollerer.

horse and log — Allen Chesser used this expression to describe the crossed trunks of two fallen trees.

house pole — A log suitable for use in a log cabin. "I can't cut into a good house-pole without resting"—Owen Thrift.

hump on — Overcome. "They [mockingbirds] put the hump on the robins, don't they?"—John Carter.

jack-o-my-lantern — Unidentified flying object visible at night. Inman Smith spoke of seeing one near Dave Mizell's house, and it was small enough to "light" on a fence post. Lang Johns saw one near an Indian mound on Bugaboo Island. Hamp Mizell saw a larger object stop above the ground. The term is appropriate, since the object was lighted and spherical.

jam — Corner. "There was a big palmetter patch growing in the jam of his fence"—Hamp Mizell.

jerk up — Discipline imposed by the Primitive Baptist church, an admonition for wrong-doing. "Old man Jack went to church that day, and they jerked him up for cussing chickens in the garden"—Hamp Mizell.

job — Push or poke. "John Mixon's wife jobbed him [a wild-cat] out of there, and the dogs run him out in the woods into a holler log, and Mrs. Mixon jobbed him to death"—unidentified speaker.

joog — To dig or to push. Referring to removing a harvest rat from its protection in a mole hill, Johnny Burch said, "I went and jooged my foot down and scratched him out. I mean he was really swift."

jower	Quarrel. Zeke Henderson, referring to William and Barbara in the ballad "Barbara Allen," said, "Look like they had a jower."
kickified	Prone to kick. Like other "-ified" words, this one stresses the disposition of a person or an animal. "The brown mule's not very kickified"—Archie Dinkins.
light'ood	Fat pine wood, used for lighting fires (light-wood, kindling). Also used as a superlative adjective. A "light'ood knot floater" was the heaviest rainfall anyone could remember.
mean	Stingy. "He was mean enough to skin a flea for its hide and tallow, and swim a mile to hell for the cracklins"—Jack Mizell.
Mistress	Widely used for "Mrs" and pronounced Miz.
muzog	To explore or look. "A good muzog or look. That's an old word in this swamp among the squatters. I use it myself sometimes"—Lone Thrift.
noseling	To sniff. "He [a bear] took his time, and went noseling about, feeding on palmeeter buds"—Allen Chesser.
open	Dog's bark. "I heard him open two or three times"—Lone Thrift.
out of chat	Hamp Mizell, describing Lone Thrift's rare unwillingness to carry on a conversation: "When he's out of chat, he's stumped and ain't a-talking. . . . When a bear killed a red sow right by his house, and it had a litter of pigs, that's what stumped him."
over	To overcome. Hamp Mizell, describing an injured young wildcat: "One was killed, the other injured, but he overed it."
passel	Can mean either a large or a small group of something, depending on the context. Usually "a whole passel."
pieded	Spotted. "Reckon it could-a-been a shorter pieded otter?"—Lone Thrift.
pinder	Peanut. From the African word *pinda*. "Coon's been eating up my pinders for a month"—Ben Chesser.
plumb	Widely used for "completely."
possuming	For "playing possum" or balking.

prairie	A term designating the open marshes of the Okefinokee, normally covered with water and aquatic vegetation.
progue	To prowl or explore, according to Jack Mizell and Tom Chesser, who spoke of a "progue about in the swamp."
pull-bone	The wishbone or "pully-bone" of a chicken.
pullikins	Lone Thrift's term for the forceps used for pulling teeth.
raisingest	Prolific, producing many offspring. "Fish is the raisingest thing in the world"—Lone Thrift.
rifle-gun	Used by some of the older swampers to designate a single-barrel flintlock gun; younger swampers sometimes used it for the common rifle such as the .22 caliber.
rock	To continue. "It was a big meeting time. It just kept in motion, you know. It rocked on up till about Friday, and there was a conference the next day"—Hamp Mizell.
scraper	A quarrelsome rascal or, in Hamp Mizell's words, a "no 'count feller."
scrimptious	Ben Chesser's term for a small amount, something scarce.
scunner	Hamp Mizell's term for a disreputable person, a scoundrel.
shim-shacking	Loafing, kidding, dilly-dallying, piddling, or wasting time, according to Jack Mizell and others.
shivers	Splinters of wood.
shot bag	A pouch worn across the shoulder and used for carrying a hunter's ammunition. "I could go out in the woods and kill any common buck or doe, skin it, and hang it on me here like a shot bag and go right on hunting half a day like I didn't have it"—Owen Thrift.
smooth	Satisfactory or productive. "My old father marked 'smooth crop' in each year [on the almanac]"—Owen Thrift.
somerset	Somersault. "Looked like he [a hog] run his head right into a stump and turned a somerset"—Lone Thrift.
spat	Slap down. "I spatted him [an alligator frog], took him to the house and cooked him"—Lone Thrift.
squirt	Moment. "It wasn't just a squirt before they raised a ruckus with him"—Owen Thrift.

strand	Swampy area such as a small branch or creek. "Have you ever been on the other side of the creek there . . . a little strand comes out of a little pond on the hill there?"—Lone Thrift.
sucking bottle	Nursing bottle. "He was crooked enough to steal a sucking bottle from a blind orphan baby"—Steve Gibson.
sweat mill	Hand-turned grist mill. "I've ground many a peck of meal or grits on what they call a 'sweat mill'"—Hamp Mizell.
swing tree	A wooden, yokelike device to which the horses are attached when engaged in plowing—Ben Chesser.
taggy	Ragged, loose, or tattered. "It has a long, taggy bloom, the cypress do"—Ben Chesser.
thrash	Thrush. A fungus infection that most often affects the mouths and throats of infants. "The baby gets thrash fever—there's yeller thrash and white thrash"—Rhoda M. Spaulding.
toll	To entice or lure. Vannie and Ben Chesser speak of "tolling the hogs" with corn to get them back from the Gap o' Grand Prairie in the drought.
trumpery	Cooking utensils and bedding. "So we had eight deer and one dog along with us, and our trumpery, all in one boat"—Allen Chesser.
turn	An armful, especially of wood, but used in a variety of contexts. "That sure was a turn of 'em [squirrels]"—Jackson Lee.
use	To inhabit or frequent an area. "That thing'd been using here for nearly two years"—Lone Thrift.
wallet	A leather pouch used to carry corn or ammunition, as opposed to a "money bag." "He carried a wallet for shot and powder, slung over a shoulder . . ."—Hamp Mizell.
water shelf	A wooden shelf located at the end of a porch on which a bucket of clean water and a bar of soap remain for the convenience of all who need to "rinse" before a meal.
whicker	Whinny or neigh of a horse.
wind	To smell. "He'll [the bear] come right there if he don't wind you"—Lone Thrift.
wood's colt	Euphemism for illegitimate child. In describing a mother

of nearly a dozen children, Rhoda M. Spaulding noted that the first six were "wood's colts" born before the woman married. Others called them "gallberry children."

working A day set aside by the Primitive Baptist church for cleaning the church building, grounds, and graveyard. "Been to the working yesterday," said Tom and Ben Chesser.

Okefinokee folk were keen observers of nature. At all seasons they were abroad in the swamp in pursuit of game and fur-bearing animals, and they navigated the expansive prairies and gloomy cypress bays, making their bivouac in spots far removed from civilization. Following the baying hounds through the piney woods, matching wits with the otter and coming to grips with the bear and the cougar, the Lees, Mizells, Thrifts, Chessers, and others saw sights that will not be seen again. They opened many pages in the book of nature that would have remained closed, even to the zoologists who visited the swamp. Their answers to questions were always well considered, and they carefully distinguished between what "some folks say" and what they considered to be the "straight story."

It took people of intelligence and imagination to follow closely the life cycles of creatures as small and elusive as the golden mouse. Those qualities of the mind and spirit are especially evident in the names the swampers chose for the living things of the swamp.

The notes that follow are gleaned from Francis Harper's own careful observations and from the swampers' recollections of their encounters with the creatures. The list is not a complete catalog of Okefinokee wildlife. The mammals and birds are well represented, but the reptiles, amphibians, and fishes have been excluded because Harper's notes on these species were not as complete.

MAMMALS OF THE SWAMP

Big Brown Bat

The big brown bat (*Eptesicus fuscus*) has been recorded only from Billys and Chessers islands. My scanty observations indicate that it roosts in the cypress bays and feeds over nearby fields. They typically appear in the evening and often enter buildings. The color variation exhibited in these bats appears to be due to age. The tips of the hairs on the upper parts are snuff-brown in the adults and bister in the immature individuals; on the under parts, buffy brown in the adults and avellaneous in the immature.

Big-eared Bat

The big-eared bat (*Corynorhinus macrotis*) is probably the least common of the bats recorded in the swamp, but specimens have been taken from a variety of places—Floyds, Billys, and Chessers islands, Craven Hammock, and from the eastern and western borders of the swamp. It commonly resorts to buildings for roosting. Sam Mizell spoke of these bats as "vampires." David Lee said a big-eared bat came into his home on Billys Island; he, too, noticed the bat's wagging of its ears. Several years ago Tom Chesser saw two of these bats following each other about in his house on Chesser's Island. When they alighted in the chimney, they made the characteristic movements with their ears. One member of the household wanted them killed, on the ground that they "raised chinches."

Pipistrelle

We have found pipistrelles (*Pipistrellus subflavus*), or "leather-winged bats" as the swampers call them, on Billys and Chessers islands, and the Minne Lake Narrows. Like the other bats of the region, they prefer sexual segregation. Some years ago I heard of a Negro near the swamp who was offering ten cents apiece for these bats. Apparently he was planning to use them for some sort of medicine or charm. More recently Raymond B. Cowles informed me that some of the Zulus of South Africa make similar use of bats.

Rafinesque's Bat or Twilight Bat

In the summer months Rafinesque's bat (*Nycticeius humeralis*) is the most common species of the Okefinokee region. Specimens were taken both in the pine barrens and over grassy or cultivated fields, often in the vicinity of dwellings. During the last half hour of daylight, they are seen at a distance of from forty to seventy-five feet. As darkness falls, however, they come much closer to the ground, so that specimens can be knocked down with a reed fishing pole. Only during the mating season (August) did we find any male specimens, thus confirming their tendency toward sexual segregation.

Francis Harper bagged a wild turkey on one of the hunts. His own inscription to this photo read: "A Cracker and a gobbler." August 1921.

Red Bat

The red bat (*Lasiurus borealis*) seems less common than any species other than Le-Conte's big-eared bat. It feeds over open ground in or near pine barrens or over streams. Just before dusk on June 13, 1922, I saw several of these bats flitting back and forth over Starling Branch where the road crosses it. Their light yellowish-red color distinguished them from other species. Mrs. Joseph Holt has captured several of this species in the past by using an old hat. Apparently the sexes are segregated out of

Here, with a local 'possum, is Alexander Stephens McQueen, who described himself as "a country lawyer, and up to the short ago the best lawyer in Charlton County, being the only one." May 1929.

mating season. All of the bats that we captured were females; we found not a single male.

Seminole Bat

The Seminole bat (*Lasiurus seminola*) is the most common species of the swamp in the winter, but in the summer it is outnumbered by Rafinesque's bat. We found this bat on Floyds, Billys, Jones, and Chessers islands, around Minnies Lake Run, Billys Lake, and Buzzard Roost Lake, and along the St. Marys River from Maclenny to Camp Pinckney. The first bats to appear in the evening seem to come from about two hundred feet and gradually descend to as low as ten feet. The Seminole bat averages somewhat smaller than the red bat, at least as far as the females are concerned.

Black Bear

The majority opinion among the best-informed local authorities is that two species of bears live in the Okefinokee: a small brown "hog bear," and a large black "cassenyie bear" or "seeny bear" (from the shrub "cassena" or "seeny," *Ilex cassine*), which is distinguished also by a white throat patch. Hamp Mizell gave the maximum weight for the hog bear at 300 to 400 pounds and the weight of the other as 500 to 600 pounds. Walter Davis also recognized these two kinds of bears, but he placed their approximate weights at 200 and 400 pounds. On the other hand, Allen Chesser and John M. Hopkins (both experienced men of the swamp) claim that only the hog bear inhabits the Okefinokee. It is true that the black bear (*Ursus americanus*) varies through two color phases—from black to nearly brown—but in both phases, white patches can be seen on the chest.

The diet of the Okefinokee bear is varied: eggs from turtles and alligators, yellow-jackets' nests, white ants, all kinds of bugs living in rotten wood, larvae and honey of ground-nesting bumblebees; bullaces (*Vitis munsoniana*), berries of bamboo (*Smilax*), saw-palmetto, "sweet bay" (*Persea pubescens*), "high-bush gallberries," and an occasional hog—as the swampers who raise this domestic animal will testify.

Beaver

Although rare to the region, the beaver (*Castor canadensis*) is known by its handiwork. Beaver dams can be found near Gum Wells, near Manor, and on Suwanoochee Creek about fifteen miles west-northwest of Fargo. In 1890 an old Negro woman, Clarissa Bisey, was startled by a beaver about six miles west of Traders Hill. Since both of them claimed right to the road, Clarissa clubbed the beaver to death. Probably the

Lucy, Molly, and Robin Harper with a bear from the Suwannee Canal. December 1935.

beaver is not able to penetrate the territory claimed convincingly by the alligator.

Cougar

When Oliver Goldsmith wrote "The Deserted Village," he saw fit to mention the "wild Altama[ha] / Where crouching tigers wait their hapless prey." His knowledge of the wildlife of the region was not so faulty as some of his critics have supposed. To this day the cougar (*Felis concolor*) is almost invariably spoken of as a "tiger" and occasionally as a "panther" in the Okefinokee region. But recent sightings of the cougar are few, for it may well be nearly extinct.

Stories of encounters by pioneer families with the "tiger" are plentiful. There was the wife of William Gunter on the Little Okefinokee who, one afternoon in 1864, went to a spring for water and was followed home by a "tiger." She barely escaped by barring the door, and the "tiger" jumped to the roof of the house and stalked from one end to the other. Her husband, meanwhile, came back from the woods with his old flintlock. He saw the animal, dropped down on his knees, and shot it off the house. It measured nine feet from tip to tip.

The last "panther scare" of record in the swamp took place at Billy Spaulding's cabin on Floyds Island in the fall of 1935. Uncle Billy saw the animal coming through the bay near the boat landing. James and Gad Roddenberry were visiting there when they heard the sound of this creature—"like a woman screaming." Both Roddenberry men were so upset that they insisted on spending the night in Spaulding's cabin.

White-tailed Deer

The white-tailed deer (*Odocoileus virginianus*), the only native ungulate of the region, is known simply as the "deer." Once abundant, in the years before the creation of the Wildlife Refuge the population was greatly reduced. The deer frequents a wide variety of habitats—hammocks, pine barrens, prairie heads, cypress ponds, cypress bays, sphagnous bogs, prairies, and watercourses. David Lee said it prefers pine swamps to cypress bays because the pine swamps offer more room for running.

James Henderson's comments on the deer are especially significant: "I've never seen any difference between the 'hill deer' and the 'prairie deer' that some folks tell about. In summer they have a small range—two to three miles; from September to January, a larger range—eight to ten miles. From about April 10 to August the deer is red; rest of the time blue. He's got a white hair and a black one; call him blue. Generally shed horns about February 1. . . . September to January is the rutting season. They have one to two fawns at a time. A yearling has perhaps one; the older ones, two. Have them once a year, April to July. A buck matures in two to three years. A doe will have a fawn at a year old, if it was an early fawn. They eat huckleberries, red bamboo [*Smilax*] berries, tupelo-gum[*Nyssa ogeche*] berries, chokerberries [*Aronia arbutifolia*], possum haws [*Viburnum nudum*]—nearly all the berries they can reach."

In one hunting season, Allen and Sam Chesser killed 144 deer. Allen said that "Black Jack [Island] was covered with 'em. We'd scarcely ever go there without bringing back six or eight." I told Tom Chesser about his forebear's large harvest of deer one day. He replied: "Yes, that's why I can't find a single one. They didn't leave none for us."

Gray Fox

Most swampers have either seen or heard the gray fox (*Urocyon cinereoargenteus*). Gad Roddenberry said that the fox first appeared in the region around 1890. William Bartram, however, makes note of them a hundred years before that. As Jim Robinson (*b*. 1854) said, foxes were simply less common in earlier days. John Prevatt said that foxes enjoyed playing together and were a sight to see as they made high leaps into the air. In earlier years fox hunts were held regularly on the eastern side of the swamp. They still seem to thrive around Waycross, where hunters let the chase go on until the fox climbs into a convenient tree or "holes up." The hounds are then called off, and the fox is left in peace. This pleasant custom seems rather general in southern Georgia.

Bryant, David, and Lem Lee with a Billys Island fawn. May 1912.

Pocket Gopher

The hills of the pocket gopher (*Geomys pinetis*) are found in sandy soil throughout the Okefinokee region and sometimes in low pine lands, but more often on fairly dry oak ridges. The "salamander" [a corruption of "sandy-mounder"], as the swampers call this creature, is not looked upon with favor. W. E. Steedley of Hebardsville noted how the animal damaged crops, particularly sweet potatoes and turnips. The natural enemies of the salamander are hawks, owls, foxes, bobcats, weasels, and the gopher snake.

Mink

The mink (*Mustela vison*) seems to drift in and out of the environs regularly. Such experienced hunters as James Henderson, Allen Chesser, and Walter Davis never met with it. Jackson Lee claimed to have caught one around the turn of the century, and the family kept it in a pen for a while. Hamp Mizell and Lone Thrift probably both described the mink, even though they said it was "something" other than a weasel. Perhaps Jackson Lee's description of 1921 is best: "Had a tail flattened out like an auter's [otter's], about four or five inches long. Seemed like it favored a auter more than anything else I know of. Had a slim body and short legs. Tail with fur, next to body, as big around as a thumb; then tapered off like a auter's tail. Colored sort of like a water rat" (*Neofiber*).

Eastern Mole

Of fairly general distribution outside of the swamp, the eastern mole (*Scalopus aquati-*

cus), or the "ground mole" as the swampers call it, has been recorded on only a few of the islands in the interior (Cowhouse, Floyds, Chessers, Gallberry, and Jones). Sam Mizell was something of a mole "specialist." He must have caught a hundred individuals, including one albino, by watching their runs, digging them out with a hoe or his hands, thrusting his fingers down behind them and flipping them out. "I knew their feed-time—right soon of a morning; from twelve to two o'clock; and late in the evening," he said. "If you saw them feeding at any other time of day—say ten or eleven o'clock in the morning—there was mighty apt to be 'weather' [rain]." They feed at night also. Their favorite foods are corn (when planted as seed), pinders (peanuts), and peas. Swampers often put coal tar on seed corn to keep moles from eating it.

Mole-shrew

In the Okefinokee mole-shrews (*Cryptotis parva*) are generally spoken of as "mole-rats" (Billys Island) or "ground-mole rats" (Chessers Island). We took our specimens in pine barrens, although there are records of shrews in other habitats. Allen Chesser found these creatures on Chessers Island under old logs, or in the ground, while ploughing or digging potatoes. On Billys Island, David Lee used to turn them up with the plough or find them in sweet-potato banks.

Star-nosed Mole

Sam Mizell discovered some live young star-nosed moles (*Condylura cristata*) in a nest

Henry Harrison Lee with a soft-shelled cooter and a pied curlew. July 1921.

above the water inside the stump of a bay tree in March 1916. In 1921 Lem Griffis showed me a specimen that he had captured and roughly stuffed in 1917. In 1924 Lone Thrift found a nest of young moles that Sam Mizell told him about: "It looked about as much like a mole as anything I ever saw. It had a long nose. They was young un's there, was four of 'em. Look like a softshell turtle's nose, with whiskers around it. It was in a nest, in a green bay stump that had been cut off in the right of way. It was made of differ'nt things, sort of like a rat bed."

Cotton Mouse

The cotton mouse (*Peromyscus gossypinus*), called the "house mouse" in the swamp, is a very common and widely distributed species in this region. It is probably the most abundant mammal of the prairie houses. It is almost entirely nocturnal and crepuscular in habits. I have never seen it abroad by day, though it is sometimes taken in buildings in the daytime, perhaps after being disturbed from some hiding place.

Golden Mouse

One of the noteworthy events of our collecting season of 1921 was the discovery of this rare and beautiful little mouse in the Okefinokee. Forest fires of recent years had almost wiped out the golden mouse (*Peromyscus nuttali*). The "little red rat," as it's known locally, prefers to live and nest in bushes and trees. In September 1922, Tom Chesser and I discovered another enemy that had been wiping out the mouse. I put my fingers into one of their nests, and al-

most simultaneously Tom sang out: "Look-a-yonder at that snake!" Just above my hand was a medium-sized black snake. It was on the same kind of hunt as we were. We "crombed the varmit," in short order and added to our collection of snakes.

Other rodents observed in the swamp included the rice rat (*Oryzomys palustris*), known as the "swamp rat"; the cotton rat (*Sigmodon hispidus*), known as the "tabbied rat," "wood rat," or "field rat"; the wood rat (*Neotoma floridana*), known as the "stick-nest rat," "slick-tailed rat," and "big white rat"; the water rat and the round-tailed muskrat (*Neofiber alleni*), known as the "prairie-rat," "water-rat," and "muskrat"; the house mouse (*Mus musculus*), known simply as the "mouse"; and the black rat (*Rattus rattus rattus*) and the roof rat (*Rattus rattus alexandrinus*), both known interchangeably as the "file-tailed rat" and the "crib rat."

Opossum

The opossum (*Didelphis virginiana*) prefers the wooded portions of the swamp and has been recorded in large numbers near Suwannee Creek, Big Water, Billys and Chessers islands, Suwannee Canal, Starling Branch, and along the St. Marys River near St. George. Jackson Lee and Allen Chesser said it likes the hammocks; but it can also be found in the piney woods, in cypress bays (especially during dry times), and in cultivated fields. Occasionally it visits the farmyards to make a raid on the poultry. Sam Mizell pointed out that the 'possum is more common outside of the swamp than on the islands in its interior and is less abundant than the raccoon. "Sambo," as some folks call him, feeds upon chickens, "roas'n' ears" (corn), persimmons, saw-palmetto berries, and fruit of any kind.

otter once was sought by trappers in great numbers. In 1922 hides of the animal brought a premium of twenty dollars each. The main enemy of the otter, in addition to man, probably is the alligator.

Otter

Although its numbers decreased in the 1920s and 1930s, the otter (*Lutra canadensis*) is generally distributed along the waterways, such as Billys Lake, the Big Water, the canal, the numerous runs through the cypress bays, and the open water of the prairies, and can be found on the Suwannee and St. Marys rivers. In the Okefinokee parlance, an otter "slide" is practically any place where the animals defecate. This may be merely a log beside any watercourse, the "sign" being frequently noted in such a situation. More commonly, according to Jackson Lee, it is some muddy spot, where the animals leave marks of scratching and wallowing as well.

In addition to its diet of fish, the species feeds upon snakes, crawfish, and field corn. Its tastes are almost as varied as the human's. Harrison Lee told about a tame otter he kept on Billys Island. The animal would eat anything, Lee said. "It had to be shut up at mealtimes, or it would come right on the table." In April 1922, a family along Hull's Creek above Camp Pinckney on the St. Marys River made a pet of an otter that became gentle almost instantly. L. B. Lloyd near Folkston took in the otter as a household pet. It played well with two children and enjoyed the playful companionship of the housecat. It ate greedily of watermelon, tomatoes, dead birds, rats, and any kind of fresh meat. As the most valuable fur-bearing animal of the swamp, the

Eastern Cottontail

The eastern cottontail (*Sylvilagus floridanus*) goes by many names in the swamp. James Henderson and David Hickox liked the name "old field rabbit" or "cottontail," whereas the Lees of Billys Island used only the latter. On the eastern side of the swamp, according to Sam Mizell, some called it the "old garden rabbit." On Chessers Island it usually was spoken of as "Riley rabbit" or simply "Riley" (reminiscent of Joel Chandler Harris's "Uncle Remus"). As Uncle Allen Chesser used to

Pearl Lloyd and her pet otter. July 1922.

say, it likes to live "out in the high woods." Henderson claimed the cottontail damaged peas and beans. David Lee added that they especially enjoyed items from the garden, such as collards and cabbage. Hunters depended on hounds to hunt "Riley" on Chessers Island. Around 1910, according to David Lee, the boys of Billys Island successfully hunted the cottontail with bow and arrow, helped by their dogs.

Marsh Rabbit

Most residents referred to the marsh rabbit (*Sylvilagus palustris*) as the "swamp rabbit," but Sam Mizell and the Chessers had their own favorite names. Mizell's was "black hare," and the Chessers' was "Barney"—a name they gave this rabbit after members of the family heard a visiting hunter use the term (perhaps he said "bunny"). More common than the cottontail, the marsh rabbit thrives in most areas of the swamp and has been found swimming by hunters' dogs. This rabbit "makes a regular rabbit squeal" when caught, Sam Mizell pointed out, and Allen Chesser noted that the favorite habitat of this species is the swamp itself: "Don't travel much out in the piney woods. Take it a dry time out on the perairie, an' them houses catch afire. Take your stand on the other side, an' about the time the fire was half through, you'd see the rabbits a-bilin' out of the house, a-skimmin' out over the perairie." The parasitic warble found in the necks of some of these is called a "wool" locally. People of the Okefinokee generally enjoyed eating both kinds of rabbits.

Raccoon

The raccoon (*Procyon lotor*) is the most abundant of the fur-bearing animals of commercial importance in the swamp. Jackson Lee speculated that there probably were at least five thousand 'coons in the swamp in 1921. Five or six members of the Lee family took about two hundred skins during the winter of 1916/17. The frogs, fishes, berries, and turtle eggs, so abundant hereabouts, make it easy for the 'coon to lead a healthy life. Other food includes berries of various sorts, such as "black bamboo" (*Smilax laurifolia*), saw-palmetto, and huckleberries, as well as fish and crawfish. Among its enemies, actual or potential, are men, dogs, alligators, wildcats, poisonous snakes, and at one time cougars and wolves. David Lee suggested that the raccoon gives birth in February, at about the same time as the bear. The largest litter Lee ever noticed was four.

Skunk

Allen Chesser and James Henderson reported that the skunk (*Mephitis mephitis*), or

Young raccoons on Billys Island.

the "polecat" as he's locally known, seems less abundant in the swamp than in former years. The pine barrens apparently constitute the principal habitat of the species, but the hammocks and other places are frequented. Jackson Lee says that they generally stay around in the pineywoods and that he has found their dens under "clay-roots," the upturned roots of fallen trees. "The polecat is found in the piney woods, in a holler log or a gopher hole. He ain't much of a feller for the water," Allen Chesser says. The natural enemy of the skunk inside the swamp, as elsewhere in much of its range, is the great horned owl; indeed, one specimen owl we took in July 1921 was redolent of "polecat."

Flying Squirrel

Found throughout the swamp, the flying squirrel (*Glaucomys volans*) is especially fond of areas where acorns can be gathered. He enjoys other nuts as well, and farmers who tried to grow pecans were unable to control these nocturnal visitors until they discovered the effectiveness of the domestic cat. Members of James Johnson's family, living near Thompsons Landing on the St. Marys, stated that a cat of theirs had caught thirty-seven flying squirrels about their place in the pecan season of 1921. On January 21, 1936, John W. Burch saw an odd combination on the same limb of a dead pine tree—a flying squirrel and a "sham-shack" or red-bellied woodpecker. The squirrel flew down in spirals to the base of the tree later, apparently in pursuit of the "sham-shack." The squirrels make a familiar squeaky sound: *tseet, tseet, tseet*.

Fox Squirrel

The fox squirrel (*Sciurus niger*) is a handsome species that was declining in numbers in the 1920s and 1930s. Harrison Lee said that when he was a boy on Billys Island back in the 1890s he could go out with his old dog for a short distance in the piney woods and get all the fox squirrels he wanted. They had practically disappeared, however, even before the cutting of the pines on this island, which began about 1922. Jackson Lee pointed out that fox squirrels generally stay around the piney woods or in the cypress ponds. They have their nests in cypresses or gums around the ponds, but do their feeding out in the piney woods. Their nests are made of cypress bark and limbs, sort of like a cat squirrel, but fox squirrels will also have nests in a dead tree, while cat squirrels prefer nesting in holes in living trees. James Henderson ventured that turpentining drove out the fox squirrel, because he did not like to have gum on his feet!

In addition to eating green pine burrs, Allen Chesser explained, the fox squirrel had rather exotic tastes: "Now talking about eating grasshoppers, there's a thing that loved grasshoppers. Also scuppernongs—any kind of fruit or grain. Ear of corn—nip out the heart—and throw the balance down. And acorns. You might bring 'em a quart of acorns, and they wouldn't eat more'n one or two before they'd be totin' all the rest off. In a day or two you'd see him going and scratching 'em up. Take him one or two, and go along about his business."

Gray Squirrel

The gray squirrel (*Sciurus carolinensis*), or the "cat squirrel" as the swampers call it, is an abundant species in the swamp. Jackson Lee mentioned securing in one day twenty-six cat squirrels with twenty-seven shots: "It was sure a good turn of squir'ls." Their favorite habitats in the swamp are the hammocks, the cypress bays, and the cypress ponds. Allen Chesser never saw cat squirrels out in the piney woods; "they're a feller that hugs the swamp," he said. David Lee said they liked the hammocks, because of the acorns and the pine mast that they find there. "There bees times when they go after the pine burrs out in the woods," he recalled. The cat squirrel resorts to holes in trees and constructs nests outside of leaves and the like. Both Sam Mizell and David Lee pointed out that the young ones, born in the spring, are always found in the hollow trees and not in outside nests which are used for other purposes. They like to eat acorns, pine mast, cypress mast (or "balls"), huckleberries, tupelo berries, mistletoe, and perhaps sweet-bay berries. The swampers are fond of hunting cat squirrels, and they prize the flesh for the table.

Long-tailed Weasel

The long-tailed weasel (*Mustela frenata*) seems to prefer living in cypress bays, branch swamps, pine barrens, and cypress ponds. It quickly ascends trees and bushes when pressed by enemies. In 1924, E. L. ("Lem") Griffis of Mixons Ferry told about finding a den of weasels in the winter of 1917. The mother weasel engaged in a severe fight with the hounds, and Mr. Griffis killed it. He took the three small ones—the size of mice—home in his hat: "I gave them milk for a few days, and then fresh meat. They grew up very fast. They stayed perfectly satisfied until I moved them out to the barn, but they did not stay there very long. They were free all the time to go where they pleased. . . . That was the last trace I had of weasels."

Wildcat

Several experienced hunters (among them J. D. Hendrix, Hamp Mizell, Newton Roddenberry, and Allen Chesser) have claimed that there are two kinds of wildcats: the "bobcat" and the "catamount." The bobcat is said to be shorter and smaller, to be "darker tabbied," and to have a shorter tail than the other animal. I tend, however, to agree with James Henderson and Jackson Lee, who say that these differences are purely individual variations, some of which may be due to age or sex. The wildcat (*Lynx rufus*) is fairly common and very generally distributed throughout the swamp. It seems to be found in practically all the surrounding territory as well. It prefers hammocks, perhaps, but it frequents a wide variety of habitats. There are records of unprovoked attacks by the wildcat upon humans. On more than one occasion, J. D. Hendrix was nearly attacked. In 1895 he was lying in wait for wild turkeys on the edge of the swamp about eight miles southeast of Waycross. He said a "catamount" stalked him to within four feet, making motions with its feet like a house cat ready to spring on a bird. Hendrix turned quickly and shot. The animal jumped high and went off a few rods to die. When I first saw the wildcat in 1922, I was surprised at the reddish brown of the animal's general appearance and at the light-colored patches on its ears. James Henderson once saw as many as four young wildcats in a litter, and he was convinced that there is but one litter a year. J. D. Hendrix observed that wildcats eat pigs, rabbits, and wild turkeys. They also are reported to have killed sheep and goats.

Wolf

The story of the wolf (*Canis lupus*) in the southeastern United States is now largely a matter of past history, unless the Okefenokee Wildlife Refuge makes it possible for the animal to breed in a natural state. At the turn of the century the species was distributed throughout the surrounding country, and it seemed to prefer the pine barrens. S. L. Davis of St. George told me that his father brought three hundred head of cattle to that region around 1855 and that within three months or so only about sixty were left, the others having been killed by wolves. Sam Mizell pointed out that wolf tracks are longer and narrower than a dog's.

Old timers I met in the second decade of this century used to speak about the abundance of black wolves (*Canis niger*) in the region before the Civil War. In 1866, when J. D. Hendrix came to the swamp, there were a few wolves that preyed upon hogs and calves. The famous hunter Obadiah Barber was said to have killed some of this species in the 1880s. Residents of Chessers and Billys islands knew of the wolf only by its howling and not by sight. Mr. W. H. Booth of Manor heard wolves on Alligator Creek at the turn of the century. He said he had seen many wolf pits when he was a boy: "Sometimes they dug pits. Sometimes they built a pen, covered over, with just a hole in top." Probably Floyds Island was the last place in the swamp where wolves were reported, and that was in 1921. The disappearance of the wolf, like that of many other interesting creatures, evidently has been brought about solely through the agency of civilized man.

Lucy Harper petting a dead wildcat. December 1935.

The Book of Genesis recounts that "out of the ground the Lord God formed every . . . bird of the air, and brought them to the man to see what he would call them." The Okefinokee folk did not take lightly their task of naming the birds of the air. Though untrained in systems of naming, they got along well with their local and regional folk names. They knew seven kinds of woodpeckers, and the one Harper called "pileated" went by five colorful names in the Okefinokee: "lord-God," "good-God," "Kate," "woodcock," and "woodchuck." Their system accounted for over ninety species. Although they did not keep lists of birds, they knew that people who lived in different parts of the swamp occasionally named birds to suit their wishes. The great blue heron (*Ardea herodias wardi*) was "po' jo" and "po' Job" to the folk of Billys Island. But the Chessers called the same bird "preacher."

The list that follows is alphabetized by the generic part of the common name and includes all the birds that Harper listed in his Okefinokee notebooks.

COMMON NAME	OKEFINOKEE NAME
least bittern (*Ixobrychus exilis*)	———
red-wing blackbird (*Agelaius phoeniceus*)	ricebird
eastern bluebird (*Sialia sialis*)	bluebird
bobolink (*Dolichonyx oryzivorus*)	Maybird
bobwhite (*Colinus virginianus*)	partridge, quail
cardinal (*Richmondena cardinalis*)	redbird, redbird-with-black-chin
Carolina chickadee (*Parus carolinensis*)	———
chuck-will's-widow (*Caprimulgus carolinensis*)	whip-poor-will, stick-far-the-white-oak
American coot (*Fulica americana*)	blue Pete
double-crested cormorant (*Phalacrocorax auritus*)	nigger goose
sandhill crane (*Grus canadensis*)	whooping crane
common crow (*Corvus brachyrhynchos*)	crow
fish crow (*Corvus ossifragus*)	jackdaw
black-billed cuckoo (*Coccyzus erythropthalmus*)	rain crow
yellow-billed cuckoo (*Coccyzus americanus*)	rain crow, barn owl
ground dove (*Columbigallina passerina*)	parrakeet
mourning dove (*Zenaidura macroura*)	turtle dove, ground dove

black duck (*Anas rubripes*)	black mallard
ring-necked duck (*Aythya collaris*)	blue bullet, puddle duck, bull duck, butter-ball, whistle-wing
wood duck (*Aix sponsa*)	squealer, summer duck, acorn duck
bald eagle (*Haliaeetus leucocephalus*)	———
common egret (*Casmerodius albus egretta*)	white crane, big white plume bird
snowy egret (*Leucophoyx thula*)	egret
Acadian flycatcher (*Empidonax virescens*)	tick bird
crested flycatcher (*Myiarchus crinitus*)	yellow-tailed bee bird, cow-driver, May-whack
blue-gray gnatcatcher (*Polioptila caerulea*)	blue mockin'
Canada goose (*Branta canadensis*)	wild goose
common grackle (*Quiscalus quiscula*)	blackbird, grackle
pied-billed grebe (*Podilymbus podiceps*)	diedapper
Cooper's hawk (*Accipiter cooperii*)	blue darter
marsh hawk (*Circus cyaneus hudsonius*)	goshawk
red-shouldered hawk (*Buteo lineatus alleni*)	frog hawk, hen hawk, chicken hawk
red-tailed hawk (*Buteo jamaicensis*)	rabbit hawk, goshawk, eagle hawk
sharp-shinned hawk (*Accipiter striatus*)	little blue darter
sparrow hawk (*Falco sparverius paulus*)	tilly hawk
black-crowned night heron (*Nycticora nycticorax*)	redeye
great blue heron (*Ardea herodias wardi*)	po' jo, po' Job, preacher
green heron (*Butorides virescens*)	Indian pullet, scoot
little blue heron (*Florida caerulea*)	blue scoggin (adult), white scoggin (imma-ture), calico scoggin (transition)
yellow-crowned night heron (*Nyctanassa violacea*)	redeye
ruby-throated hummingbird (*Archilochus colubris*)	hummer
white ibis (*Eudocimus albus*)	curlew, white curlew, pieded curlew (immature)
blue jay (*Cyanocitta cristata*)	jaybird, blue jay
killdeer (*Charadrius vociferus*)	deerkill
eastern kingbird (*Tyrannus tyrannus*)	bee bird, bee martin
belted kingfisher (*Megaceryle alcyon*)	catbird
swallow-tailed kite (*Elanoides forficatus*)	fish hawk
limpkin (*Aramus guarauna*)	———
common loon (*Gavia immer*)	———
mallard (*Anas platyrhynchos*)	English duck
purple martin (*Progne subis*)	martin
eastern meadowlark (*Sturnella magna*)	lark, field lark
hooded merganser (*Lophodytes cucullatus*)	frog duck, bullet

mockingbird (*Mimus polyglottos*)	mockin'
common nighthawk (*Chordeiles minor*)	speed bat, bull bat
brown-headed nuthatch (*Sitta pusilla*)	tomtit
white-breasted nuthatch (*Sitta carolinensis*)	quilt
Baltimore oriole (*Icterus galbula*)	————
orchard oriole (*Icterus spurius*)	————
osprey (*Pandion haliaetus*)	fish eagle, eagle
barred owl (*Strix varia*)	deer owl, swamp owl
great horned owl (*Bubo virginianus*)	horn owl
screech owl (*Otus asio*)	scrich owl, freeze owl
eastern wood pewee (*Contopus virens*)	tick-bird
eastern phoebe (*Sayornis phoebe*)	tick-bird
water pipit (*Anthus spinoletta*)	————
king rail (*Rallus elegans*)	prairie chicken
redstart (*Setophaga ruticilla*)	————
robin (*Turdus migratorius*)	robin
spotted sandpiper (*Actitis macularia*)	sweet, mud-knocker, peewinker
yellow-bellied sapsucker (*Sphyrapicus varius*)	sapsucker
leser scaup (*Aythya affinis*)	keel
shoveller (*Spatula clypeata*)	pipebill
loggerhead shrike (*Lanius ludovicianus*)	loggerhead, bull's ear, bull hawk, bullhead
sora (*Porzana carolina*)	————
common snipe (*Capella gallinago*)	————
Bachman's sparrow (*Aimophila aestivalis*)	————
English sparrow (*Passer domesticus*)	sparrow
roseate spoonbill (*Ajaia ajaja*)	pink curlew
starling (*Sturnus vulgaris*)	————
wood stork, formerly wood ibis (*Mycteria americana*)	flinthead, ironhead, mule-head, baldhead, wood gannet, salt-water crane
chimney swift (*Chaetura pelagica*)	chimney swallow, chimney sweeper
summer tanager (*Piranga rubra rubra*)	umparil
blue-winged teal (*Anas discors*)	————
arctic tern (*Sterna paradisaea*)	————
black tern (*Chlidonias niger*)	sea gull
brown thrasher (*Toxostoma rufum*)	swamp thrasher
yellow throat (*Geothlypis trichas*)	————
hermit thrush (*Hylocichla guttata*)	chapbird, trotter
wood thrush (*Hylocichla mustelina*)	————
tufted titmouse (*Parus bicolor*)	————
rufous-sided towhee (*Pipilo erythrophthalmus*)	red-eye joree, bullfinch, jo-e
turkey (*Meleagris gallopavo*)	turkey gobbler

water turkey (*Anhinga anhinga*)	———
red-eyed vireo (*Vireo olivaceus*)	———
white-eyed vireo (*Vireo griseus*)	———
black vulture (*Coragyps atratus*)	cyarn [carrion] crow
turkey vulture (*Cathartes aura*)	buzzard
black poll warbler (*Dendroica striata*)	———
Cape May warbler (*Dendroica tigrina*)	———
hooded warbler (*Wilsonia citrina*)	———
parula warbler (*Parula americana*)	———
prothonotary warbler (*Protonotaria citrea*)	———
Swainson's warbler (*Limnothlypis swainsonii*)	———
yellow-throated warbler (*Dendroica dominica*)	———
whip-poor-will (*Caprimulgus vociferus*)	whip-poor-will
American woodcock (*Philohela minor*)	snipe
downy woodpecker (*Dendrocopos pubescens*)	sapsucker
hairy woodpecker (*Dendrocopos villosus*)	———
ivory-billed woodpecker (*Campephilus principalis*)	ivory-bill
pileated woodpecker (*Dryocopus pileatus*)	lord-God, good-God, Kate, woodcock, woodchuck
red-bellied woodpecker (*Centurus carolinus*)	shamshack, ramshack, chadcherry
red-cockaded woodpecker (*Dendrocopos borealis*)	sapsucker
red-headed woodpecker (*Melanerpes erythrocephalus*)	white shirt, jerry coat, shirt tail, whiteback
Carolina wren (*Thryothorus ludovicianus*)	house wren, fence-dodger, shakybag

Francis Harper was a full-time naturalist, always on duty, making notes—sometimes scholarly, sometimes trivial, but notes forever pertinent to his interests. In 1964 he attempted to compress his notebooks into manuscript form. His observations from Chessers Island alone were over two hundred single-spaced pages. The abundance of material is not surprising, since this place on the eastern border of the swamp became headquarters for most of his trips after 1922.

This abridged version of the notes from Chessers Island reveals Francis Harper's joyous discovery of the folk who became his Okefinokee neighbors and lifelong friends. Here we see clearly not only his genuine love for the swampers but also his growing conviction that their inevitable departure from the "land of trembling earth" was a lamentable event. These entries are momentary glimpses into the mind and heart of a man who virtually became a part of several swamp families. So it was perfectly natural for Harper, eventually, to refer to himself as a "Cracker." More important, the swampers found the reference perfectly natural.

June 18, 1922
Letter to a friend in Ithaca.

We have had our home here in a "hammock" for nearly a week. [Harper's companions are Miles Pirnie and A. H. Wright.] Our four tents are spread beneath the shade of moss-draped live oaks. We are well protected while working, eating, and sleeping, from the mosquitoes and gnats, and they are not very bad even outside. . . . Specimens are fast accumulating, some of a particularly desirable sort. The Chessers come and sit around camp, giving us their own local names of plants and animals, and imparting various highly interesting bits of swamp lore.

We make fairly frequent trips (13 miles) to town [Folkston], where we can buy "loaf bread," and so haven't yet had to make any "cawn braid." But we are feeding high on some of the Chessers' good cane "sorup," sweet taters, and fresh beef. Their "maters," "pinders" [tomatoes, peanuts], and some of their other crops got "nigh drownded out" this year, however.

Last evening we went out with Tom Chesser on his daily task of finding and driving home their herd of cattle, which wander off several miles through the piney woods. . . . To hear Tom holler as he drives home the cattle will thrill anybody that has any feelings at all.

Yesterday I all but stepped on a good-sized cottonmouth moccasin coiled up among thick grass, but saw it at the last moment and leaped about a mile beyond. It never lived to tell the tale, for I broke me off a "light-'ood knot" and "crombed" it.

July 3, 1922
Letter to a friend on Long Island.

We hear that fine old Billys Island, our headquarters on every previous trip, is nearly all cut off now, and so we are not very joyous over the prospect of seeing it. We will doubtless stay on Chessers Island most of the summer. It is a very pleasant place, too; its isolation and primitiveness approaching that of Billys Island of old. I wish you could listen to old Mr. Chesser tell us about his bear fights of earlier days, while I copy them down in full, in his own quaint and humorous vernacular. . . . The baby of the family is about five years old, and an unusually bright and cute one. The other day, when we put some question to her, she brought down the house by responding, "That's a mighty deep subjec." The young ones are constantly bringing in some bug or rat or Indian arrowhead or bit of pottery. The other day I photographed one of the medium-sized girls wielding the "battlin' stick" during laundry operations.

July 8, 1922

Yesterday was our biggest day yet for the present season—a trip across Grand Prairie to Buzzard Roost Lake and return. Six of us

setting out in three boats around 8:30 A.M. Hard poling to Sego Lake, better thence to Monkey Lake, and some hauling (or rather pushing) the short remaining distance to Buzzard Roost Lake. It was particularly interesting to see this piece of water as the scene of Allen Chesser's big fish drive of the 'gators in bygone days. . . . On the way out Tom paid me the compliment of remarking: "Mr. Harper look like he done some polin' before." . . . So we made the long pole home without trouble, except for Miles' falling out once, and my going with him. The others waited for us several times, and we kept them in sight about as far as the "Bear House."

July 9, 1922

Last night there was a little "sing" up at the house. Tom, Cato [Kate], Julia, and Roxie forming the chorus, and singing out of a "four-note book." First they seem to get the tune by going over the song, singing various combinations of the notes "*fa, mi, sol, la.*" Tom made all sorts of funny excuses and delays before getting under way, until Cato in her impatience clapped him on the shoulder with a scolding "Tom Chicken." Then soon Tom would say, "Let's hunt another one." . . . He sat with the book on his lap, legs crossed, while the others looked over his shoulder, some standing, some sitting. I flashlighted them in the act of singing "Sons of Sorrow."

July 22, 1922

Ben was telling me this evening how his father used to holler, especially in the early morning during fall and winter, when they got up before day (say four o'clock) to grind cane. They used to grow enough cane to keep them grinding a couple of months. Three years ago the syrup brought as high as $1.50 per gallon, but recently only about 30 cents. Hence less cane grown.

August 21, 1922

Hardy Johns, of Moniac—there is a swamp character. It was indicated yesterday the moment he came from his house, ready to pilot us to Ellicotts Mound, for he bore with him his trusty gun, inseparable companion of your true swamper. Gun on shoulder, he bothers little with other equipment. A voluble talker, it took a little time to catch on to his curious lingo. And some of the uncommonest-looking eyes I have ever gazed at—I can hardly say *into*. For when facing you directly, he seems to be looking and talking off to one side, somewhat out of the corners of eyes and mouth. Also a sort of set, glassy expression to those

Washday meant wielding the "battlin' stick." Roxie Chesser launders as Mattie and Vannie watch from the doorway. June 1922.

pale blue orbs, as if they might also be sightless. A lank, tall, and hardy ranger of the Okefinokee; fifty-one years old, and traveling in and about the swamp most of his days. . . .

I had no idea that we could get within a mile of the mound, as we did, with the car. In dry weather you could get within a hundred yards, as Hardy Johns said. We drove from Moniac perhaps three miles, on the east side of the river, over as fair a road as we had traveled that day—which, however, was not saying a great deal. We paused at

Bentons Ford over the river. There three of us set out afoot, crossing the river skittishly on a log nearly a foot under water (me with the Graflex, binoculars, and raincoat hung on to me). Thence through open country (mostly cut-over pine-barrens), across a branch, where we waded again through the tupelo gums in water over our knees, thence through more open country to the '58 post, and around a cypress pond to Ellicotts two mounds. The principal (northern) one has two light'ood sticks thrust into it by later surveyors. The other is not over a

A Chesser Island family singing "Sons of Sorrow" at evening. July 1922.

rod away. Each is a slight elevation, say a foot and a half, and about eight or ten feet in diameter. They have been there long enough for oak-runner to become established, though it was not noticed in the lower surrounding ground, consisting of intermediate and wet pine barrens. The slight mounds themselves are not much to look at, nor to arouse emotion except from reflection on the man who made them and the part they have played in history. [In 1796–1800, Major Andrew Ellicott of Lancaster, Pennsylvania, erected a mound of earth near the source of the St. Marys River. This marker was decisive in settling border disputes between Georgia and Florida.]

August 26, 1922

Uncle Allen recited the words to a song composed by his father, William Tennyson Chesser, about an old maid who was attempting to gain the favor of Allen's brother, Buck:

THE OL' MAID'S COURTSHIP

I'll tell you of a courtship
An' how it first begun
Between ol' granny's daughter
An' Little Ellen's son.

She permanates so nicely [promenades],
Her actions is complete,
She's the finest of the family
When she gets in her silver teeth

August 29, 1922

Upon learning that I was going to camp for several days alone on Grand Prairie, Uncle Allen gave me a final admonishment:

"Now, Francis, when you get out yonder on Grand Perairie all by yerself, if you meet up with one of them bears, *stand up to him!*" I replied: "That's what I aim to do, Mr. Chesser." However, from the point of view of my own composure, perhaps it's just as well that no such meeting took place.

2:30 P.M. At Gap o' Grand Prairie a preacher [heron] flapped across the gap ahead . . . in the direction of No. 1 Island. . . . A gloriously independent feeling. I have made the gap evidently without going far from the main trail, though I was somewhat uncertain between the Mossy House and the Stick-nest Rat House.

5:00 P.M. Land to camp on Mitch Mizell's camp house. Tom Chesser arrived a little after dusk with five wood ducks he had shot in the gap as he came through late this afternoon. Two we had for supper, and I nearly finished one off by myself. . . . He also brought with him a little of my baggage left over from morning. [*March 10, 1964:* For over forty years I have had a warm glow of friendly feeling toward Tom for this visit of his to me at Mitch Mizell's camp house. He was not duck hunting, really, but was concerned that I not go astray in my journey through the swamp. In later years I twitted him over his uncertainty about whether a greenhorn such as myself might be lost in the bewildering expanse of Grand Prairie. I recall his response: "Well, I was sort of studying about that."]

August 30, 1922

When Tom left a little after breakfast, I had only a few of the wild things for neighbors—blue-tailed skinks searching through the dead leaves outside or coming in under the front door; a ground lizard, a new discovery in this habitat; an occasional visiting Kate and Downy [pileated wood-pecker and downy woodpecker]. I have fixed up rather luxuriously for a swamp camp—8' x 11' tent, with mosquito netting in front and back; my bed-roll on a mattress of *Tillandsia* [Spanish moss]; a table improvised of a box upturned over four stakes, on which I do my skinning and writing, prac-tically free from disturbance.

August 31, 1922

Last night I woke with something inside my pajamas. Turning on the flash, I fairly shud-dered to see a long fat millipede (or round centipede?). I rousted him out in a hurry. . . . I have often remarked that the longest two seconds in my life were those required to grab the flashlight and turn it on. [Re-flecting on this experience more than forty years later, Harper said that it was a more terrifying experience than any he had ever had with wolves, bears, 'gators, cotton-mouths, or other varmints.]

September 1, 1922

Mitch Mizell's camp house. While watch-ing the sweet potatoes boil for breakfast, I note that mosquitoes scarcely appear except toward and after dark, and then they are not numerous. Likewise a few belated yellow flies come late in the day. No ticks found on me so far.

I have seen sunsets in various lands and upon the sea, but never such a one as this evening. I had gone out in the boat for a couple of buckets of water from the 'gator hole, and as I rounded the side of the "house," the celestial splendor struck me fairly agape.

First in the east I had noticed a focus of light streamers at the intense blue cloudless horizon, and then I saw that it was but a replica of streaming rays from the sun be-hind clouds in the west. The rays were faintly visible clear across the zenith as they curved to the eastern focus. The con-densation or focusing of these rays in the east, like a reflection of the west, is beyond me. . . . Those glorious turrets and battle-ments of clouds with burnished rims!

And when I managed to push along out to the 'gator hole, there it was doubled—another sunset in the pool! Those noble words of Maurice Thompson, quoted by Will Henry in his Okefinokee paper, came vividly to mind: "The silver green and gold of water and leaf and bloom, the blue of the stainless sky and the sombre gray of the cypress colonnades were finer than any col-ors that Titian mixed or Raphael saw in dreams."

[The brothers Maurice and Will Henry Thompson, distinguished authors and natu-ralists, visited the Okefinokee first in 1866. The passage noted by Harper probably is from Will H. Thompson's "Deep in the Okefinokee Swamp," *Forest and Stream* 85 (May 1915): 301.]

September 4, 1922

Made some miserable burnt and greasy bread in a hurry for supper, and then got a late start for the evening's hunt at Buzzard Roost. The crowning joy, however, was the specimen of the king rail—our first one from the swamp itself. It jumped from the prairie along the "water-road"; I let my push-pole fly, grabbed the gun, drew more or less of a bead, and pulled the trigger. Down then came his kingship with a big splash in the water-road ahead.

September 8, 1922

Yesterday Tom and Ben went to the "workin" at Sardis Church—an annual affair in which a large proportion of the congregation takes part. The women folks scrub up the floors and the meetinghouse generally, while the men hoe the weeds out of the graveyard and fix it up.

September 10, 1922

My week on Grand Prairie was a wonderful experience. I had never before been quite by myself for such a length of time, and I would have felt the loneliness the more, except that I was extremely busy and having extraordinary luck. . . . I have been alone here for a little more than two weeks, except for the Chessers, who make very good company, and with whom I take my meals (at ninety cents per day)—hog and hominy, hot biscuits, some of the famous Chessers Island cane syrup, and sweet potatoes, along with some occasional beef, duck, squirrel, or other fresh meat. . . . I could be having the time of my life here.

September 17, 1922

Steve Gibson spoke earnestly as I walked toward the Chessers': "Look-a-hyere, I don't know what to make of you, whether you just got good grit or don't know no better, spending a week out yonder on the perairie by yourself. . . . I wouldn't go out there by myself and stay among all them alligators and things for a thousand dollars." As I came up to the house, dressed for the rail journey northward, Uncle Allen Chesser looked me over and said: "Well, that's the first time I ever see you with a choke rag on. Now you're Mr. Harper, no more Francis."

May 22, 1929

Spent over an hour with Col. A. S. McQueen, talking over swamp matters. Allen Chesser is dead! Since this spring. A tremendous and deeply felt loss to me. Hamp Mizell is over by Suwannee Lake now, and Sam Mizell is working for the Hebards in Florida. . . . The rest of the Chessers are still on their island. Tom and Ridley are married; Ben's not. . . . As for Lem Griffis on the lower side of the swamp, he's a "prosperous bootlegger." According to McQueen, there is some uncertainty as to the Chessers' attitude toward me since the publication of "Tales." ["Tales of the Okefinokee," *American Speech* 1 (May 1926): 407–20]. Apparently they took some exception to the presentation of the dialect.

May 25, 1929

Out along canal from Camp Cornelia. New peace comes to my soul in these fair bits of prairie, tiny as they are. A cooling breeze, too, on a torrid day. Away from the turpentine-scarred piney woods.

June 5, 1929

Bugaboo Island. I asked Lang Johns, "This is Wednesday, ain't it?" He replied, "Yes, providing it don't rain nor frost today. If it rains, it'll be a rainy day. If it frosts, it'll be a frosting day." Seated on the Indian mound on the farther island, I could almost imagine myself in the Okefinokee of bygone days. Only the low turpentine boxes and

Steve Gibson's hammering in putting up a workers' shack on the island adjoining slightly mar the illusion. These piney woods seem to possess the spirit of everlasting things.

June 6, 1929

Daybreak in the piney woods. Up at the unusual hour of five, aroused by Steve Gibson and his boys who are arising and hollering. The birds are more vociferous now than later in the morning. The bobwhites pipe, the joree calls and sings. The cardinal sings *oleet, oleet*, a woodpecker drums, the pine warbler trills. . . . The camp breakfast gets underway earlier than usual. The smoke rises pretty straight in the still air, as the fellows squat by the fire, frying hoe-cake or stirring the raw white potatoes they have just dropped in a skillet of grease. Some sit around inactive.

June 11, 1929

Lang Johns says to plant Irish potatoes on the fourteenth of February or on full moon of August. Plant them any other time, and you won't make as much of a crop by a third or a half. Lang breaks into a song playfully, like a square dance. He says it is a favorite with the Chesser children:

Take this lady by the hand,
Lead her like a pigeon.
Make her dance the merry dance,
Till she loses her religion.

Lang said people around here, especially the Chessers, made up songs to make multiplying easier—all the way up to the number twelve. All these gems I heard about the campfire with the Cornhouse Creekers.

May 24, 1930

Chessers Island. Camping in the hammock, after eight years, with memories. . . . Unheard-of hordes of mosquitoes driving us indoors at dark. The last "young uns" of the Chessers—Mattie and Vannie—now young women. None of their brothers and sisters (except Ben) now on the island, as several were last year. Ben and the "young uns" were cordial like old times. . . . Ben and Tom stick mainly to farming—a far pleasanter life than turpentining.

May 25, 1930

Last night Mattie showed me handwritten copies of "Lassie Mohee" and "The Soldier Boy" which they had copied from similar transcripts in the hands of Mitch Mizell's girls. "The Soldier Boy" is new to me. Mrs. Harry Chesser told me this morning that she heard and knew "Lassie Mohee" and "Barb'rie Allen" when she grew up around Starling Branch.

This morning I photographed Mrs. Chesser, Vannie, Harry, and Harry's children shucking and shelling corn at the corn crib. They still make their own meal and grits here. Yesterday afternoon Jean and I did some hoeing with the young uns in the cornfield, to compensate in part for the loss of Vannie's time from the work in the morning. [Vannie had helped the Harpers locate some botanical specimens.]

May 29, 1930

After breakfast I went over to Tom's house and took some photographs of his folks, especially of little Wade, the apple of Tom's eye. By the time we left, about 11 A.M.,

Corn shucking, like many of the farm tasks, was a family affair on Chessers Island. May 1930.

Tom invited us to dinner. The two hours till dinner time we spent in a walk down through the piney woods on the island, botanizing and photographing.

Dinner was grand—fresh snap beans and squash from the garden, boiled rice and pork gravy, Irish potato salad, baked sweet potatoes, fried bacon, hot biscuits, cornbread, Chessers Island cane syrup, coffee (with sugar), and *huckleberry pie*! Jean and I ate a powerful lot. At first only Tom and his two oldest kids sat down with us, and eventually, after considerable urging, one of his sisters-in-law joined us. The second sitting doubtless consisted of Tom's wife and mother-in-law with some smaller children.

After dinner Vannie and Mattie and Jean played "fox and geese" with grains of corn on a sort of checker board marked on the floor of the porch. I photographed the whole party, then some of Tom's curios stuck on the side of the house. One of these was a conch shell, brought by W. T. Chesser from Liberty County.

During the talk this morning, when Tom mentioned "playpretties" [referring to his children's toys], Jean said he must be the first person besides myself she had ever heard use the word. Then I added how we were bringing up our "brats" on Okefinokee words, and that evidently tickled Tom.

After dark this evening, in the rain, Mrs. Chesser, Mattie, and Vannie came and sat with us in the tent for over an hour. Mattie said she didn't mind my printing the ballads I have gotten from her. Mrs. Chesser reminisced considerably, especially as I read some of the songs from Hamp Mizell. She said Allen sang both "Jaybird Setting on a Hickory Limb" and "Old Joe Clark."

Allen quit frolicking and playing . . . when he joined the church. She said, however, that "Brother Owen" [Owen Gibson, the Hardshell Baptist pastor] likes to hear a

fiddle sometimes. One of the girls said that when Uncle Allen was getting paralyzed [shortly before his death], he said he wished he could try a banjo to see if he could still pick it with his fingers.

July 23, 1931

Mrs. Allen Chesser said that three of Granddaddy (W. T.) Chesser's sons—Buck, Bill, and Tom—were in the Confederate Army, but left and came back here. They stayed out in the swamp—probably out in the "prairie houses"—and rations were "toted" to them. Before they came back from the army, they threw their guns into the river. When they arrived home, they were barefooted and nearly naked. Family members would watch the slough [toward the mainland] to see if anybody was coming after the three Chesser boys. Granddaddy Chesser made his sons some shoes. [On March 12, 1940, Harper noted an echo of this incident. Tom Chesser described how homefolk would signal to those in hiding. The deserters would deposit deer or other game at some place where their relatives could get it and leave, say, grits in exchange. Neither party saw the other. Tom said deserters stayed "all about the swamp," particularly in the area northwest and west of the island.]

April 10, 1932

Appalling forest fires all about the last few days, even in the heart of the Okefinokee. Around Bee Gum Prairie and Trout Lake, going out on the "hill" around the Fence Pond and Chesser school area; also on Floyds Island and along the canal; perhaps on Billys and Honey islands. . . . Tom

Chesser, who had gone out in the edge of the prairie west of the north end of the island, said he had to race for his life and was really scared; blazing hanging moss was blown ahead of him and set fire there. All of us did some "stringing" until midnight on Friday. We burned a narrow strip of grass and undergrowth to form a barrier against the spread of the approaching fire. This is an effective procedure in the piney woods. There seems to be very little attempt to beat out a fire directly. In the bays no "stringing" is possible, and little or nothing can be done.

April 12, 1932

Both Ben and Harry Chesser declared emphatically that they had never seen "such a sight in their lives"—the swamp as it now is. Even the "houses" on Grand Prairie were burnt up. . . . This past week of fires has had a fairly numbing effect on the senses: hard to settle down to work, to accomplish anything, to write notes. Numbers of houses and barns were burned and destroyed between the swamp and Trader's Hill a couple of days ago, as a strong west wind blew the blaze swiftly across the land.

Ben and Harry Chesser walk toward Gap O' Grand Prairie, where a devastating fire is taking its toll of timber and wildlife. April 1932.

April 17, 1932

A visiting lady, unused to swamp ways, asked Tom if he would "holler." He indicated gently that the present moment was not exactly a propitious time. (It never is when strangers are about.)

April 11, 1933

On our way to the island yesterday, it was an amazing and refreshing experience to find how green the country looks after last year's drought and fire. Even a mile or two out on the "hill," where everything on and near the ground was consumed or fire-blackened, there is a good green growth of grass and other ground plants. . . . Tonight Mattie and Vannie Chesser sang "Barbara Allen" and "Little Mohee" while doing the dishes.

March 28, 1938

A party of seven of us from the Philadelphia area (Margaret and Comfort Cary, Lloyd Cadbury, Spencer Coxe, Sam Brown, Jean and I) arrived in the early afternoon at Chessers Island, to spend several days of Easter vacation. We had come by way of Camp Cornelia, where there was a huge, long pile of pine logs, partly sawed up. We learned, to our amazement and dismay, that the logs had come from the south end of Chessers Island and were being used for cooking the rations at the adjacent camp of a colored C.C.C. outfit. Jean protested as soon as possible to F.D.R., and the vandalism was forthwith stopped, after irreparable damage had been done to some twenty-five acres of nearly primeval pine timber in the Okefenokee National Wildlife Refuge—

only a few months after its establishment and opening.

March 31, 1938

At dusk tonight Jean and I went over to Tom's for a delicious Chessers Island supper: rice; stewed canned pork (home-made), with bones, gravy, and dumplings; field peas; rutabaga greens; hot biscuits; black grape jelly; and coffee. We ate and ate, and could hardly stop. Tom and the six youngsters sat down with us, but Ivy, in the old Okefinokee style, waited on us and finally seated herself to eat after we were through. Jean remained with her while the rest of us adjourned to the porch for a grand time of talking, reminiscing, and swapping recent news.

January 12, 1939

Very sad news the other day—Uncle Owen Gibson died last month, and there were a thousand people at his funeral [according to a letter from Iva Chesser]. There could scarcely have been a more worthwhile or lovable man in Charlton County. No one can even remotely take his place in the hearts of the community.

August 22, 1944

I was quite anxious, with only a couple of days left to make a phonograph record [for the Library of Congress] of Tom's driving the cattle home. About 5 P.M., with the help of little Lester, Tom gave a wonderful performance, driving the cattle down from the Second Dreen toward the homeplace. The hollering is exemplary.

Ben Chesser and his family. March 1938.

The cows presently passed by our location on the roadside, with the bell producing its pleasant Okefinokee tinkling and Tom continuing with his music so pleasurable to those whose senses are attuned to the many delightful sounds, sights, and fragrances of the piney woods. After he had gotten a little past our stand, he turned to call out, "Is that all?" This, too, was recorded for posterity.

August 26, 1944

Harry took us back to Steve Gibson's in his truck. Meanwhile, I had the best visit and most cordial talk with Harry in years. I remarked that he had been a good friend for twenty-three years, and that about the best turn he ever did me was to introduce me to Chessers Island. Steve Gibson embarrassed me a bit by repeating to Harry what I had told Steve—how touched I had been in 1921 at seeing Harry give his mother a kiss in greeting after not having seen her for some weeks or months.

August 28, 1944

We reached Washington a little after ten on Tuesday morning, and hastened to the Library of Congress, where the records we had carried by hand were played before Botkin [Benjamin A. Botkin, head of the Archive of Folk Song]. . . . The Music Division was evidently well pleased with our results, limited though the records were in quantity. Previously they had had nothing really comparable with the Okefinokee hollering. . . . When I mentioned a wish for F.D.R. to have a chance to listen to the records, Mr. Spivak said at once that they would be glad to make up a disk with selec-

tions on it and send it to him with my compliments. Botkin, inquiring into my plans and wishing to "promote" a book on Okefinokee folks, suggested that I send him an outline of the projected work. He expressed some confidence in being able to get the required support.

January 17, 1951

Chessers Island for once was apparently completely devoid of human life. Only a couple of friendly hounds greeted us at Tom's. Ivy's said to work in the school lunchroom in Folkston, and the younger children are going there to school. I get increasingly depressed on the island in recent visits. The young pines are growing up thick all around our cabins and shutting off the view; the porch planks rotting; termites perhaps at work; the generally miserable swamp management by the Wildlife Service; my own increasing general pessimism about the passing of the picturesque old-timers. . . . Hamp Chesser says young Bill writes from Korea about waking up in the morning and finding four or five of his buddies frozen to death about him. We share a general disgust with the incompetent government of our country.

January 18, 1951

From Waycross we rolled on southward along the familiar old dirt road [toward Suwannee Lake], pretty small now, and over numerous plank bridges over the branches. After lunching at one of the branches, we went on to Uncle Lone Thrift's old place, only to find it occupied by other people. At Hamp Mizell's old place [Suwannee Lake] we first encountered Leo Barber, husband of

Little Rhodie, and great grandson of the famous Obadiah Barber. Though we had never met before, he knew of me. At the kitchen door was Little Rhodie, with a glad smile, now the mother of six children. Then they called Aunt Rhodie out, who gave me welcome. . . . Leo seems an upstanding fellow, worthy of marrying a Mizell.

January 19, 1951

Soon after we got back to Camp Cornelia, Tom Chesser knocked off work, and we followed his spic-and-span new pick-up truck along the Old Swamp Road to Chessers Island. The Chessers are comparatively thriving—Tom with a steady government job (though temporarily hazarded by his refusal, as a good Hardshell, to work on Sundays), Ivy with her job at the school cafeteria, and only the two youngest boys at home to feed. Ivy seems much better in health than in past years.

I told Ivy not to make a fuss over our supper—she didn't have to for a Cracker like me, and George Cooley, as a Yankee, wuzn't wuth it! But we had fried chicken, rice, mashed potatoes, string beans, hot biscuits, coffee, and Chessers Island cane syrup. . . . It was good to be with the Chessers again and to talk over old times.

NOTES ON A
VANISHING BREED

A Postscript by Delma E. Presley

NOTES ON A VANISHING BREED

Harry Chesser lives today on a small farm in Charlton County, Georgia, within hollering distance of his former swampland. He has remained near the land of his forefathers. This is *the* Harry Chesser, son of Allen Chesser, grandson of William Tennyson Chesser. This is the man who hunted and fished with Francis Harper, who served as his guide and companion. Francis Harper said that Harry performed his greatest deed in the summer of 1921. It was then that Harry took Francis home with him to meet his father. Thereafter Francis Harper considered the Chessers to be his Okefinokee family, and their island eventually became his headquarters.

When I saw Harry Chesser at the end of the summer of 1978, he had been living away from the swamp for nearly half his life. He had begun harvesting a crop of hay for the winter, his eighty-second on this earth. He was ready for autumn, and he seemed impatient with the lingering warm weather. I explained that I had come to talk about the Okefinokee folk of this volume.

"They're all dead and gone—the real ones are," he answered slowly. It was not the last time he would say those words that afternoon on his front porch. We sat and looked at Harper's photographs of scores of swampers. He helped in various ways—by identifying persons and objects in the pictures and by correcting bits of misinformation I had. The afternoon slipped by quickly as we talked and laughed, all the while enjoying a steady breeze that swept across the shaded yard.

Harry Chesser is not given to nostalgia, and he says he is glad times have changed. He enjoys laborsaving devices on the farm and in the home, and he is grateful to be able to hear and see news of the world without leaving his living room. But he is not altogether pleased with the attitudes of people today.

"They got more *convenience* now. When I was a boy, I never dreamed I'd have what's in my house now. But life was better in some ways back yonder. So much difference as there is between black and white.

"People don't act like they are civilized, as much as they did back then. They do things now, and they don't want you to find it out. If they get what you got, they're happy. They think that if they can do that, they'll be sitting on top of the hill.

"Back then people would visit. They'd go every weekend, somewhere, and they'd visit. But now, folks don't go at all. They got a much better way to go—cars and roads—but they don't go at all."

Harry Chesser is amused by much that has been written about the swamp. To him the Okefinokee is neither a place of mystery nor a land of spectacle. Promoters and writers who "build up the swamp are just trying to make something out of nothing. They want to make the swamp seem different from what it is. Now they got the Refuge. They got a big name, got it advertised. And people will go in there and see what they've already seen, maybe. But the good thing to do is just to go and see Chessers Island. That's it. Just see the island and the swamp. That's enough."

A practical man, Harry Chesser says he realized that "living wouldn't be natural" on an island surrounded by rangers and sightseers. He made the break quickly before the swamp fell into government hands, and he maintains that he has never regretted the move.

But one of William Tennyson Chesser's grandsons tried to keep his inheritance. Tom Chesser, Harry's cousin, for two decades refused to bargain with the U.S. Department of Interior. Portions of Harper's "Chessers Island Journal" allude to Tom's stubborn independence. Tom wanted to rear his children as he and his father had been reared, and he did just that. Through 1958 he maintained his home on Chessers Island. His wife, Iva, supplemented his income as a swamp guide by working at the public school in Folkston. For years their children had urged them to move into a home with modern conveniences nearer town, and Tom and Iva eventually gave in. For 104 years Chessers had lived on Chessers Island; in 1959 there were none.

Pulling up roots from his birthright, Chessers Island, was the most traumatic experience Tom could recall. In 1969 he told Andrew Sparks of the *Atlanta Journal-Constitution Magazine*: "I mortally hated to leave. I stayed out there three weeks by myself. I pouted that long before I decided to follow the bunch. Every fellow was for it but me. . . . When I moved, I couldn't sleep for three or four nights, smelling that paint, and I couldn't breathe in those tight rooms. But the longer I stayed out, the better I like it now."

On October 25, 1977 Iva Chesser and three dozen others who share that family name gathered at the old homeplace on Chessers Island. They were joined by over two hundred guests who had come to hear a speech by Congressman Ronald "Bo" Ginn. The occasion was the dedication of a restored Chessers Island farmstead, known to all as "Tom Chesser's place." Now thousands of visitors each year walk the grounds, view the buildings, and learn the lessons of "self-reliance." The title of Ralph Waldo Emerson's famous essay has become the theme of the restoration. Maintained by the Department of Interior, the Chesser place is open to the public throughout the year.

Long before Tom Chesser gave up his island, Harrison Lee left Billys Island. The year was 1937, and it seems that the authorities went about their sad task with understanding. Harrison wanted assurance that the old family graveyard would be preserved and protected. The government has kept its word. A chain-link fence surrounds the plot. Visitors to Billys Island usually enter the swamp through its southwestern gates at Fargo, Georgia, near the Florida state line. Most who make their way up the Suwannee River to the homeland of the Lees are impressed by the silent testimony of this simple, neatly kept spot of ground.

Hamp Mizell's side of the swamp continued to be the abode of the swampers for nearly two decades after the wildlife refuge was created. Hamp's daughter Rhoda, or "Little Rhodie" as she was called, married Leo Barber, grandson of the legendary Obadiah Barber. They remained on her father's property, which bordered government land. Granted, the Barbers found it difficult to maintain their older methods of farming. But the Barbers endured, and they proudly began yet another generation of Okefinokee folk.

The Leo Barbers stayed at Suwannee Lake until 1955. Their decision to leave then was influenced little by government regulations. The Barbers were victims of the great fires of that year. In March 1955 Rhoda apologetically wrote to Francis Harper, knowing he would regret their decision: "I will not write anymore about it, for I know you will feel as I do about it. We can still see the fire light from here at night as it burns in the heart of the swamp. . . . I hope you will understand us leaving Suwannee Lake. It was very heartbreaking to me, but seemed the only thing we could do. I miss it very much but am very well satisfied here now."

Even though most swampers accepted their leaving as inevitable, not all agreed that the government gave them fair treatment. Some complained that the Department of Interior offered less than the market price for condemned lands. Others on the borders of the swamp angrily criticized the park rangers who restricted the movement of livestock that occasionally wandered into the refuge for grazing. Hogs and cows in particular were prone to disregard the "posted" signs. There are stories of deep grudges between swampers and government employees. There are also tales of bloodshed.

Old timers especially have not forgotten the case of Oliver Thrift. The local historian of Ware County, Georgia, Liston Elkins, tells the story of

Thrift's crime and punishment as though it happened yesterday. It is one of those vivid memories common to those whose roots are in the swampland.

Liston Elkins was editing the *Waycross Journal-Herald* at the time, and he had known the old swamper Oliver Thrift for most of his life. They had fished and hunted together on the northern side of the swamp. They also had shared some happy moments together in the company of their mutual friend Hamp Mizell.

On the surface, at least, the facts of the Thrift case were simple: Oliver Thrift murdered two employees of the federal government who had rebuked him for killing the bears that had been ravaging his small herds of cows and pigs. Despite previous official warnings that he could be jailed as a violator of federal regulations, Thrift continued to protect his livestock as his forefathers had done—with his shotgun. The trial was an uncomplicated affair, and there was no appeal. Oliver Thrift was found guilty of murder and was sentenced to life imprisonment on June 14, 1946.

Although the facts speak for themselves, they fail to tell what Liston Elkins regards as the real story. At heart the Oliver Thrift episode reflects the attitudes and psychology of many frontiersmen who were victims of a society that had changed radically during their lifetime. The old swamper poignantly revealed what many of us mean when we use the word "dignity."

Now Oliver Thrift lived about two miles from Hamp Mizell's place, as the crow flies. Around his two-room house was a picket fence. Lined up across the top of that fence were dozens of bear skulls. The arrangement was Oliver Thrift's diary, so to speak, for each skull reminded him of a certain year or special circumstance of his long life in the swamp. He was just as proud of his collection as an earlier Chesser, Mizell, or Barber might have been.

The ranger whom Thrift murdered was named Bryant Crews. As Elkins recounts the story, "Bryant Crews was a ranger or patrolman who was living on Cowhouse Island. He wasn't known too well around the north end of the swamp where this murder happened. He was working with another boy who was with the government. I believe his name was Joe Martin. Well, when Oliver killed Martin, he knew that Crews had seen him. So he had to get rid of them both."

Even though Martin was employed by the government, he also happened to be Thrift's neighbor and cousin. So when Martin reported Thrift's bear-killing activities to the authorities, Thrift felt betrayed.

Liston Elkins continues, "This tells you something about the simple faith those guys had in their friends. As long as you let them believe in you—as long as you don't cross them up—they're your friends. But try to cross 'em up, and you're likely to get shot.

"I was with the F.B.I. when they arrested him. We drove up to his house. The agent had ants in his pants. He thought Oliver would go out his back door and into the swamp. There wasn't but two steps between the house and the swamp. Sheriff Johnson said, 'Just let him alone now. Just let him alone. If we slip up on him, somebody will get shot. Oliver will respect us if we come up there as he expects people to come visiting him.'

"We got up to the front yard and parked, and Mrs. Thrift came out on the front porch. The sheriff said, 'Mrs. Thrift, is Oliver home?' She answered, 'Yes. He's in bed.' The sheriff asked, 'Will you tell him I want to talk to him?' She said, 'Yes, sir.' In two or three minutes he came out. He was wearing long johns. He'd been asleep.

"Oliver knew what the story was then. He was a crafty old rascal. The sheriff said, 'Now look. We think you can help us with the murder of Bryant Crews. And how about getting your clothes on, and let's go to town.' Oliver said, 'Just give me a little time, Sheriff.'

"Then that F.B.I. guy really did have a fit. He just knew Oliver could easily walk out of his back door and into the swamp, and we would never see him again. But the sheriff told the agent to take it easy, because he knew that Oliver was a man of his word.

"Well, directly Oliver came out wearing his overalls, and he was barefooted as usual. On the way to town, the sheriff told him frankly that he knew Oliver had shot Crews and Martin, that he had the information. And so Oliver told us exactly what had happened. He didn't lie about it.

"When we got to town, I told Oliver, 'Before they carry you over to your cell, I want to run over to the office and get my camera. I want to get a good picture of you.' I told him that we weren't going to try him in the *Journal-Herald*, that he needn't worry about that. I said, 'You're a person that's known all over South Georgia, and I'd love to carry a picture.' He said, 'It'll be all right.' I got the camera and I took a picture of him with his bare foot in the chair. The gun was across his knee. The sheriff stood beside him, but the F.B.I. man wouldn't appear in the picture. So after I'd made a couple of shots, Oliver said to me: 'Would you do something for me, Mr. Liston. I'd like for my wife to have one of these pictures.' I told him I'd see that it was done immediately.

"I carried a print out to her within a few days. It was an eight-by-ten print. They had a boy about seventeen years of age who had just made a good crop.

I was congratulating him on it. And I said, 'By the way, have you all been in to see your Daddy?' He said, 'No, and I want to go see him.' I said, 'Call your Momma.' Then I told Mrs. Thrift, 'Get your Sunday dress on now, and I'll carry you to town and let you see Oliver. I'll bring you back out when you're ready.' (It's about twenty miles out there.) She said, 'Well, that will be wonderful!'

"So I brought them to town to the sheriff's office. I told the sheriff to call me when they were through, and I'd take them home. The sheriff said, 'No, you needn't do that. I've got other plans.' And you know what that rascal did? That sheriff, as I later found out, went to a hotel and arranged a room for Mrs. Thrift and her son. After they saw Oliver, they went back to the hotel and spent the night. The next day they went to see Oliver again, and then the sheriff drove them back home.

"I went into the courtroom that morning of his trial, and Oliver was seated at a defense table. He had on shoes, and I'd never seen him with shoes on in my life. And he was dressed up, wearing a store-bought suit of clothes. I didn't recognize him to start with. I went over and spoke to him. I said, 'Oliver, I don't know what to say to you, but if you ever had one friend, I'm it. I understand the circumstances surrounding your situation at your farm, but I don't know if a jury ever will or not.'

"Oliver Thrift received a sentence of life imprisonment. But it didn't mean anything more to him than if he'd been sentenced to go to church on Sunday. He didn't show any emotion at all, and he never complained.

"Nobody ever heard much from Oliver Thrift after that. People seemed to think that the old swamper had done what *he* had to do, and they knew the law had done what *it* had to do. It sounds crazy, but a lot of people felt that Oliver Thrift was just as right as the law was.

"Word was that he made a model prisoner, and he served his time without incident. After the required years had passed, his time drew nigh for a parole hearing. But he became terribly sick, and a petition was circulated for an early release. He did come back home, but about the last we heard from Oliver Thrift was that he was dead and gone."

As I think about Liston Elkins's story, I remember Harry Chesser's comment: "They're all dead and gone—the real ones are." This book has been about the "real ones." They are a vanishing breed and soon will be extinct. No one is more aware of this fact than one of Francis Harper's early companions in the swamp, Will Cox. This native of Cowhouse Island used to call the sets for swamp frolics. He now lives in south Georgia, midway between his boyhood home and Waycross.

In the winter of 1979 when I talked with Will Cox, he was looking forward to seeing the swamp in April when it reaches its peak of beauty. He keenly regrets the passing of the swampers, but he takes pleasure in knowing that the swamp will endure. Will Cox remembers Francis Harper as one of his best friends, because Harper was one of the swamp's best friends at a time when it had more than enough enemies:

"We did everything we could to destroy it. We skinned alligators until we like to drove every last one off. We killed bears, otters, foxes, and almost got rid of them. We went after the cypress and cut down three thousand acres of trees. I was a part of all that. We didn't know any better.

"But the old swamp came back. The animals came back. The trees came back. You wouldn't know where the trees were cut.

"The Okefinokee is God's work. Man couldn't destroy it, and now it is as beautiful as it ever was. It is the most beautiful place on earth. I will do everything I can to make sure it stays that way for as long as the world lasts."

SELECTED WORKS BY FRANCIS HARPER

Francis Harper published approximately 135 articles, monographs, and books on the subjects of faunal zones, botany, conservation, amphibians, reptiles, birds, quadrupeds, the Eskimo, the Montagnais, early American naturalists, and folklore. Brief biographies of Harper by Ralph Palmer appear in *The Auk*, vol. 90, no. 3 (1973), pp. 737–38, and in the *Journal of Mammalogy*, vol. 54, no. 3 (1973), pp. 800–801. Harper's collected papers are on file in the Kenneth Spencer Research Library at the University of Kansas, Lawrence. The list that follows includes only works that concern the Okefinokee.

"Alligators of the Okefinokee." *Scientific Monthly*, vol. 31, no. 1 (1930), pp. 51–67.

"A Biological Reconnaissance of the Okefinokee Swamp: The Birds" (with A. H. Wright). *The Auk*, vol. 30, no. 4 (1913), pp. 477–505.

"The Chuck-will's-widow in the Okefinokee Region." *The Oriole*, vol. 3, no. 2 (1938), pp. 9–14.

Diary of a Journey through the Carolinas, Georgia, and Florida in 1765–66 by John Bartram, and Travels in Georgia and Florida in 1773–74 by William Bartram. Philadelphia: American Philosophical Society, 1942.

"Distribution, Taxonomy, Nomenclature, and Habits of the Little Tree-frog (*Hyla ocularis*)." *American Midland Naturalist*, vol. 22, no. 1 (1939), pp. 134–49.

"A Dweller in the Piney Woods." *Scientific Monthly*, vol. 32, no. 2 (1931), pp. 176–81.

"The Florida Water-rat (*Neofiber alleni*) in Okefinokee Swamp, Georgia." *Journal of Mammalogy*, vol. 1, no. 2 (1920), pp. 65–66.

"The Frog with an Alligator's Voice." *Naturalist Magazine*, vol. 19, no. 2 (1932), pp. 92–94.

"The Mammals of the Okefinokee Swamp Region of Georgia." *Proceedings of the Boston Society of Natural History*, vol. 38, no. 7 (1927), pp. 191–396.

"Okefinokee Swamp as a Reservation." *Natural History*, vol. 20, no. 1 (1920), pp. 28–41.

"The Okefinokee Wilderness." *National Geographic Magazine*, vol. 65, no. 5 (1934), pp. 597–624.

"Records of Amphibians in the Southeastern States." *American Midland Naturalist*, vol. 16, no. 3 (1935), pp. 275–310.

"Report of an Expedition into the Okefinokee Swamp." *Bird Lore*, vol. 14, no. 6 (1912), pp. 402–7.

"A Season with Holbrook's Chorus Frog." *American Midland Naturalist*, vol. 18, no. 2 (1937), pp. 260–72.

"A Sojourn in the Primeval Okefinokee." *Brooklyn Museum Quarterly*, vol. 2, no. 4 (1915), pp. 226–44.

"A Southern Subspecies of the Spring Peeper (*Hyla crucifera*)." *Notulae Naturae* (Academy of Natural Sciences of Philadelphia), vol. 27 (1939), pp. 1–4.

"Tales of the Okefinokee." *American Speech*, vol. 1, no. 8 (1926), pp. 407–20.

The Travels of William Bartram. Naturalist's Edition. New Haven: Yale University Press, 1958.

"A Voice from the Pines." *Natural History*, vol. 32, no. 3 (1932), pp. 280–88.

SELECTED ARTICLES AND PAMPHLETS

Cothran, Kay L. "Talking Trash in the Okefenokee Swamp Rim, Georgia." *Journal of American Folklore*, vol. 87 (1974), pp. 340–56.

Coulter, E. Merton. "The Okefenokee Swamp, Its History and Legends, Part 1." *Georgia Historical Quarterly*, vol. 48 (1961), pp. 166–89.

Cypert, Eugene. "The Effects of Fire in the Okefenokee Swamp in 1954 and 1955." *American Midland Naturalist*, vol. 66 (1961), pp. 485–503.

Elkins, Liston. *Story of the Okefenokee.* Waycross, Ga.: Okefenokee Swamp Park, 1972.

Gorham, Louis [Charles Gorham Barney]. "Trembling Earth." *Argosy*, vol. 68 (1911–12), pp. 33–46, 298–309, 527–35, 708–22.

Harper, Jean Sherwood. "Collecting Folk-Songs in Okefinokee Swamp," *Vassar Quarterly* (February 1933), pp. 6–10.

Harper, Roland M. "Okefinokee Swamp." *Popular Science Monthly*, vol. 74 (1909), pp. 596–614.

Pendleton, Louis. "In the Okefenokee." *The Youth's Companion*, vol. 68, nos. 3506–11 (1894), pp. 343–87.

Presley, Delma E. "The Crackers of Georgia." *Georgia Historical Quarterly*, vol. 60, no. 2 (1976), pp. 102–16.

Scoville, Samuel. "Life in a Cheerful Swamp." *World's Work*, August 1929, pp. 58–61.

Thompson, Maurice. "An Archer's Sojourn in the Okefinokee." *Atlantic Monthly*, vol. 77 (1896), pp. 486–91.

Thompson, Will H. "Deep in the Okefinokee Swamp." *Forest and Stream*, vol. 85 (1915), pp. 298–302, 337–39.

Walker, Laura Singleton, and Sara Singleton King. *About "Old Okefenōk."* Waycross, Ga., 1947.

Wright, Albert H., and A. A. Wright. "The Habitats and Composition of the Vegetation of the Okefinokee Swamp, Georgia." *Ecological Monographs*, vol. 2 (1932), pp. 110–232.

————, W. D. Funkhouser, and S. C. Bishop. "A Biological Reconnaissance of the Okefinokee Swamp in Georgia: The Reptiles." *Proceedings of the Academy of Natural Sciences of Philadelphia*, April 23, 1915, pp. 107–92.

Bell, Vereen. *Swamp Water*. Boston: Little, Brown, 1941. Now available in a Brown
     Thrasher edition from the University of Georgia Press.

Brunvand, Jan Harold. *The Study of American Folklore*. New York: W. W. Norton, 1978.

Burt, William H., and Richard P. Grossenheider. *A Field Guide to the Mammals*. Boston:
     Houghton Mifflin, 1968.

Cary, Margaret M. *Sugar Down the Wind*. Lancaster, Pa.: Science Press, 1943.

———. *Wilderness Peace*. Mount Holly, N.J.: 1944.

Coulter, E. Merton. *Georgia Waters: Tallulah Falls, Madison Springs, Scull Shoals and the
     Okefenokee Swamp*. Athens: Georgia Historical Quarterly, 1965.

Emrich, Duncan. *Folklore on the American Land*. Boston: Little, Brown, 1972.

Ewan, Joseph. *William Bartram's Botanical and Zoological Drawings*. Philadelphia: American
     Philosophical Society, 1968.

Fagin, N. Bryllion. *William Bartram: Interpreter of the American Landscape*. Baltimore:
     Johns Hopkins Press, 1933.

Hebard, F. V. *Winter Birds of the Okefinokee and Coleraine: A Preliminary Check-list of the
     Winter Birds of the Interior of Southeastern Georgia*. Georgia Society of Naturalists
     Bulletin no. 3, pp. 1–97.

Hopkins, John M. *Forty-five Years with the Okefenokee Swamp: 1900–1945*. Georgia Society
     of Naturalists Bulletin no. 4, pp. 1–75.

Huxford, Folks. *Pioneers of Wiregrass Georgia*. Vols. 1–5. Waycross, Ga., 1951–1967.

Izlar, Robert Lee. "The Hebard Lumber Company in the Okefenokee Swamp: Thirty-six
     Years of Southern Logging History." M.S. thesis, University of Georgia, 1971.

Laycock, George. *The Sign of the Flying Goose: The Story of Our Natural Wildlife Refuges*.
     New York: Anchor, 1973.

McQueen, Alexander S. *Clubfoot of the Okefenokee*. New York: Pegasus, 1938.

———. *History of Charlton County*. Atlanta: Stein and Day, 1932.

———, and Hamp Mizell. *History of the Okefenokee Swamp*. Clinton, S.C.: Jacobs, 1926.

Mayer, F. E. *The Religious Bodies of America*. St. Louis: Concordia, 1961.

Mays, Louis B. *Settlers of the Okefenokee*. Folkston: Okefenokee Press, 1975.

Meanley, Brooke. *Swamps, River Bottoms and Canebrakes*. Barre, Mass.: Barre Publishers,
     1972.

Needham, James G. *The Life of Inland Waters*. Ithaca, N.Y., 1916.

Nixon, Edgar B., ed. *Franklin D. Roosevelt and Conservation: 1911–1945*. Vols. 1–2. Hyde
     Park, N.Y., 1957.

Palmer, Ralph S., ed. *Handbook of North American Birds*. Vols. 1–3. New Haven: Yale
     University Press, 1962, 1976.

Rawlings, Marjorie Kinnan. *South Moon Under*. New York: Scribners, 1933.

Russell, Franklin. *The Okefenokee Swamp*. New York: Time-Life Books, 1973.

Thomas, Bill. *The Swamp*. New York: W. W. Norton, 1976.

Utley, Francis Lee, and Marion R. Hemperley, eds. *Placenames of Georgia: Essays of John
     H. Goff*. Athens: University of Georgia Press, 1975.

Wells, Charles F. *Condensed History of Baptists: Mainly Georgia Primitive Baptists*. Macon, Ga., 1963.

White, Newman Ivey, ed. *The Frank C. Brown Collection of North Carolina Folklore*, vols. 1–7. Durham: Duke University Press, 1952–65.

Wright, Albert Hazen. *Life Histories of the Frogs of the Okefinokee Swamp, Georgia*. New York: Macmillan, 1932.